BOOMING BRANDS

Harsh Pamnani is a renowned business storyteller and brand expert. He partners with businesses to develop powerful story banks—curated collections of compelling stories that leaders can use in both internal and external communications to grow their mindshare and market share. He has authored several best-selling books and articles on brand building, which have appeared in top-tier publications like *CNBC*, *Forbes*, *The Economic Times* and *The Financial Express*.

Harsh has worked with a range of organisations, from unicorn startups like FirstCry and Icertis, to think tanks like the World Bank and TiE, to corporates like Deloitte, Cognizant and HSBC.

Harsh has shared his expertise and experience through speaking engagements at prestigious institutions like TEDx (six times), Josh Talks, IIT Bombay and IIM Ahmedabad. He teaches startup branding at MICA Ahmedabad.

Harsh is an alumnus of XLRI, Jamshedpur and IET-DAVV, Indore. For more information about Harsh and his work, please visit www.harshpamnani.com. You can get in touch with him via email at harshpamnani@hotmail.com or connect with him on LinkedIn at https://www.linkedin.com/in/harshpamnani/

Praise for Booming Brands, Volume 2

'India's first-generation entrepreneurs, most of them riding on the vehicle of digital technology, are transforming India's consumer and market landscape, at times dramatically, and at times, ubiquitously. In this collection, Harsh Pamnani energetically and purposefully brings to life the trials, tribulations and successes of a dozen-odd founders who are reshaping domains, marketplaces and paradigms in the country. This collection of diverse and trailblazing stories from PolicyBazaar to Zoomcar to Quikr offers valuable lessons to students and practitioners of business and management.' **Sunil Kant Munjal, Chairman, Hero Enterprise**

'The inspiring journeys of some of the youngest brands of India, articulated in the second volume of *Booming Brands*, are an excellent read, and Harsh has weaved a narrative that delves into the heart of these pulsating brands.' **Harsh Goenka, Chairman, RPG Enterprises**

'Brands are an intrinsic part of our everyday journey, and some become more proximate if they resonate values and purpose that we hold dear. Harsh has captured that essence of the "brand building" process for Indian brands, some of which have already come of age and others that will soon make a stronger footprint. A very useful, analytically rich, and step by step guide to building brands "the Indian way".' **Suresh Narayanan, Chairman and Managing Director, Nestlé India Ltd**

'Harsh Pamnani made a signal contribution to marketing literature in India with *Booming Brands,* Volume 1. It is our good fortune that he is back with a sequel covering some of the hottest contemporary brands ranging from PolicyBazaar to Epigamia. His carefully collated stories clearly indicate that those who predicted the demise of brands wrote their obituaries far too prematurely.

More power to those who build strong brands from India, and to their indefatigable chronicler, Harsh Pamnani.' **Rishikesha T. Krishnan, Director, IIM Bangalore and former Director, IIM Indore**

'Harsh has done a fabulous job in articulating the insights emerging from the journeys of each of these powerful brands. Having helped incubate a consumer healthcare startup, I understand the value of these learnings for budding next-gen entrepreneurs and the inspiration the ones on the edge could draw. A great read and one to keep.' **Samina Hamied, Executive Vice Chairperson, Cipla Ltd**

VOLUME 2

BOOMING BRANDS

INSPIRING JOURNEYS OF 11 'MADE IN INDIA' BRANDS

HARSH PAMNANI

First published in hardback by TV18 Broadcast Ltd in 2020

First published in paperback by Westland Business, an imprint of Westland Books, a division of Nasadiya Technologies Private Limited, in 2023

No. 269/2B, First Floor, 'Irai Arul', Vimalraj Street, Nethaji Nagar, Alapakkam Main Road, Maduravoyal, Chennai 600095

Westland, the Westland logo, Westland Business and the Westland Business logo are the trademarks of Nasadiya Technologies Private Limited, or its affiliates.

Caricatures designed by Prashant Arts

ISBN: 9789357766500

10 9 8 7 6 5 4 3 2 1

Typeset by Jojy Philip, New Delhi 110 015
Printed at Nutech Print Services-India

To my father, Surendra Pamnani, for becoming my
first source of inspiration
To my mother, Kanchan Pamnani, for inspiring me
to dream big

In memory of
Late Dr Manohar Chandwani, IET-DAVV, Indore,
an excellent motivator and mentor

Contents

Introduction

Many entrepreneurs aspire to create new businesses with the dream of making a fortune. When we look optimistically, with a population of more than a billion people, India makes for a market of great opportunities. But when we look from an execution perspective, India is one of the toughest markets to crack. It has diverse cultures, languages, demographics, buying power and consumer behaviours. Moreover, today's consumer is becoming more demanding, new technologies are disrupting established business models, the number of marketing channels are increasing, and the attention span of the consumer is decreasing. In such a crowded, complex and competitive market, building an admirable brand from scratch has become one of the toughest tasks for entrepreneurs and marketers.

Though the business environment and market trends in India are rapidly changing, the referable material on brand building has not evolved at the same pace. Most of the material taught in business schools and books available in the market cover examples and case studies of international players. Brand-building strategies that worked in developed markets like the USA may not be applicable in emerging markets like India. Some excellent material has been written about age-old Indian brands. Still, due to factors like liberalisation, increasing employee attrition rates and digital media, brand-building strategies that were effective in the past are slowly becoming obsolete today.

I was curious about how admirable brands are created in today's tough world and in complex markets like India. I read a few biographies, but they were about business leaders who had started businesses long ago. Many of these books covered the journeys of entrepreneurs from rags to riches but didn't dwell on how they created powerful brands. While some of the books on marketing were great reads, they mainly looked at international examples as case studies.

To satisfy my curiosity, over the weekends and after office hours, I started attending sessions at The Indus Entrepreneurs (TiE), which is the world's largest non-profit organisation focused on fostering entrepreneurship. The TiE team liked my passion and offered me a two-year opportunity to make an impact on the entrepreneurial ecosystem in India. By the end of this opportunity at TiE, I realised that I was not ready to become a full-time entrepreneur.

I discussed my situation with one of my mentors at TiE, and he gave me a piece of advice that I hold dear. He spoke of two famous people in the world of cricket. One, Sachin Tendulkar, who played in the field, and the other one was Harsha Bhogale, who doesn't play but understands the game, its players and their strategies and talks about them. He said, 'You don't want to become an entrepreneur, who goes and plays like Sachin in the business field, but you are passionate about businesses and entrepreneurs, you may like to become someone like Harsha Bhogale in the field of business.'

That one piece of advice changed my vision, and it gave me a positive role model and a source of inspiration. I found that Harsha Bhogale writes articles in newspapers and magazines. I also decided to write for business publications. It took me almost one year to get my first article published in a reputed business publication. Starting from that one article, I have written over 50 articles in most of the renowned business publications, including *Forbes* and *The Economic Times*.

After getting a grip on my writing skills, I decided to write a book. I had met many entrepreneurs, marketers, professors and students who had expressed that there are many new-age Indian brands that are getting noticed at the global stage, but their journeys have not been documented. Looking at this void, I felt I could write a book that could be used by people who are interested in understanding how new-age 'Made in India' brands have been created.

It was vital for me to cover popular brands, get backing from a reputed publisher, and testimonials from influential leaders. I created my book-writing plan taking my personal resources, such as time and money, into account and then chose booming brands in various niches. Then, I created a structure of stories covering the 'why', 'how' and 'what' of the journeys of selected brands. I pitched to multiple brands, and luckily the founders of 11 leading Indian brands, including BookMyShow, Shaadi.com, Zomato and Paper Boat, agreed to give me their valuable time and a few of the highly respected names in the world of business and academia including Harsh Mariwala and Ronnie Screwvala gave me their testimonials. In addition, CNBC, one of the biggest names in business media, agreed to publish my book.

My book was released at my alma mater, XLRI, by Professor Sharad Sarin, one of the senior-most marketing professors in India, who has been teaching at XLRI since 1976, along with Professor Ashis Kumar Pani, Dean of XLRI. In due course, my book was appreciated by Amitabh Kant, CEO of NITI Aayog, Government of India, as well as Prakash Javadekar, Union HRD Minister, Government of India. Over time, many other influential business leaders and academicians praised my book, and the word spread. And then came one of the most memorable moments of my life when I got an opportunity to meet my role model—Harsha Bhogale.

The journey of *Booming Brands, Volume 1* and the great response that I received from those from the business fraternity, as well as readers, motivated me to write another volume, covering the inspiring journeys of 11 more 'Made in India' brands. There are many excellent books and case studies written by both international and Indian authors on the topics of marketing, brand management and the journeys of entrepreneurs. The purpose of this book is not to substitute or supplement any of the available material. My mission is to bring forward the remarkable adventures of a few entrepreneurs who built something out of nothing and have contributed immensely to build the entrepreneurship momentum in India.

Please note that this book contains brand journeys originally written between 2019 and 2020 and republished in 2023. While the stories are based on a particular timeline and do not reflect the latest developments in these brands' journeys and the lives of the individuals mentioned, the book provides valuable insights into how these new-age brands were created from scratch, how they achieved popularity in crowded and competitive markets, and how the entrepreneurs behind them identified new opportunities to develop million-dollar businesses. These timeless lessons from the hard-earned successes of these brands from multiple industries and domains can help you carve out your own journey and brand strategy.

policybazaar.com
Compare. Buy. Save.

Shaping the market for financial security

Walt Disney once said, 'All the adversity I've had in my life, all my troubles and obstacles, have strengthened me. You may not realize it when it happens, but a kick in the teeth may be the best thing in the world for you.' There are numerous examples of successful businesses that were created by people who turned their adversities into achievements. This is one such story.

Yashish Dahiya had been living in Europe for a decade. In 2008, he came to India to visit his parents. One day, as he was going through his father's investments, he found that insurance agents had cheated him. Insurance agents had misled Yashish's father, a retired army officer, into investing in policies that were dependent on the stock market's performance. He had been told that his money would be safe, as if in a fixed deposit but with better returns.

Between 2003 and 2008, the stock market in India had been booming and Yashish's father received decent returns. But in 2008, the stock market crashed, and his father's hard-earned savings of ₹20 lakh lost significant value. Surprisingly, his father was unaware that while investing in these policies, he had paid commissions of around ₹6 lakh to the agents and that he also had to pay surrender charges to insurers as the agents had got the policies changed within three years.

Unfortunately, there was widespread misinformation and malpractice in the market. Investment-cum-insurance policies that were not suitable for customers but provided better commissions to agents were pushed enthusiastically. In contrast, health and life insurance policies that were good for customers were not promoted due to insufficient commissions offered to agents. Yashish felt exasperated with this state of affairs.

Since childhood, Yashish had witnessed many of his loved ones suffer due to a lack of adequate health cover. When he was ten years old, his uncle had died, and he had seen the hardships the family had to face in its aftermath. Another one of his uncles had burnt his leg and was devastated since he had dreamt of joining the Indian Army. Moreover, financial liabilities became a burden for him. Then, Yashish lost a colleague to cancer, and his colleague's family had to sell their house and car to meet their basic financial needs. He was aware that it was due to a lack of transparency and rampant mis-selling by agents that people were reluctant to buy insurance policies despite their many benefits. India, in fact, was one of the least insured countries in the world.

With the mission to change India's insurance industry for the better, Yashish decided to stay back in the country and build an insurance-related startup called PolicyBazaar. In its first decade, PolicyBazaar faced many ups and downs but emerged as India's largest online insurance aggregator and distributor, with a market share of over 90 per cent.

Over the years, PolicyBazaar has won over 50 national and international awards for its innovative business model, marketing efforts and customer-centric approach. These awards include India's Top and the World's Leading Fintech Innovator, Best

Fintech Marketplace and the Best Corporate Brand. Backed by many marquee investors, including Softbank, Tencent, Temasek, Tiger Global, Intel Capital, Inventus Capital Partners, Chiratae Ventures, Info Edge, Premji Invest, Wellington Management, Ribbit Capital, Steadview and True North, PolicyBazaar is considered one of the most valuable startups in India. It is also one of the very few profitable consumer internet companies from India.

THE BEGINNING

While growing up, Yashish was not sure of the career he wanted to pursue. So when the time came, he gave around 20 entrance exams, including the Combined Defence Services entrance exam, IIT-JEE and CAT. Fortunately, he passed all the exams and ended up doing electrical engineering from IIT Delhi, followed by an MBA from IIM Ahmedabad (IIM-A). When he graduated, the average monthly salary for an IIM-A graduate was ₹20,000. Around this time, his sister was preparing for entrance exams, and Yashish decided to teach her and 20 other students. He enjoyed teaching and earned ₹25,000 in the first month by working for just two to three hours a day. He decided to continue giving private home tuitions and rejected the college placement.

Though Yashish was enjoying teaching, his parents wanted him to get a job. Owing to his parents' concerns, he joined Illinois Tool Works, a company that manufactured and sold industrial packaging products. Initially, he had no interest in working there and joined forty-five days late. But over time, his mind changed. When the CEO asked him what role he wanted, Yashish immediately asked for the toughest job and was sent to the market development and analytics department in Rajkot.

He grew rapidly within the company and became the youngest business unit head in a span of two-and-a-half years. Though he was doing well in his career, he had an unfulfilled dream. While studying at IIT, he had attended a session by an INSEAD professor and wanted to fulfil his longtime desire to study at the institute. After working for four years, he went to France to pursue his second MBA at INSEAD.

Yashish started his corporate journey in Europe as a management consultant with Bain & Company. Later, he went on to become the Managing Director of Ebookers, a leading online travel aggregator in Europe, which was later acquired by Orbitz, a company now part of Expedia. Then, between 2005 and 2008, Yashish founded First Europa, a global online insurance broker. Unfortunately, the venture didn't succeed.

In 2008, when Yashish found how some insurance agents had misled his father, he decided to investigate the problem and asked many people about the insurance products they had purchased. He found that not even 2 per cent of them were aware of the benefits of their insurance plans. Digging further, Yashish found that 97 per cent of the insurance products sold in India were investment-cum-insurance products that provided agents with large commissions, and just 3 per cent of the products were pure health and life insurance products that helped investors deal with emergencies and unforeseen circumstances.

To understand the insurance agents' point of view, he spoke with many agents and found that each agent could only sell one or two policies per month. He realised that these agents spent the whole day travelling and going door to door. If they were not even able to make a ₹10,000 commission per policy, then it became difficult for them to survive. The policies that were beneficial for customers would give commissions of about only ₹1,000, and they weren't able to make 10 to 20 transactions in a month. Hence, the agents were interested in pushing products that were beneficial for them rather than for their customers.

His analysis led him to understand the needs of the market, and Yashish decided to start a platform to list the features and the pricing of various insurance products. He joined hands with his friends Alok Bansal and Avneesh Nirjar, and laid the foundation of PolicyBazaar in 2008.

THE BRAND NAME: POLICYBAZAAR

Interestingly, meaningful and memorable brand names can be created by simply linking common words in the right order. The brand name PolicyBazaar, for instance, was created by linking two popular words, 'policy' and 'bazaar'. The name is self-explanatory, stands out in the crowded insurance market and has an excellent recall value.

As Yashish was developing a marketplace for insurance policies, he felt that the name PolicyBazaar would be a good fit. Luckily, the domain name Policybazaar.com was available, and Yashish picked it up. The name has worked in favour of the brand; because of it, Yashish explains, 'We do not need to educate a significant section of society about who we are and what we stand for, which also translates into monetary savings for us.'

BUSINESS LESSONS

Many essential business lessons can be learnt from the evolution of PolicyBazaar.

When things get hard, work harder

Back in 2008, insurance customers in India were facing tough times. Instead of taking insurance to deal with uncertainties and emergencies, people were considering insurance policies as tax-saving investment products due to a lack of awareness. Consumers felt detached from the insurance industry, and there was a high lapse rate of policies. In fact, insurance companies made huge profits from policy surrender charges.

From a market perspective, 2008 was not a good year to start a new business. The world was reeling from the impact of the global financial crisis, and corporates were tightening their purse strings. The venture capital industry in India was not mature like it is today, and the few investors who were present in India were either not investing or were not interested in PolicyBazaar. Yashish's savings were depleting, and there was no money to pay the employees. He struggled for several months, and it was challenging for him to keep his team intact and motivated.

Yashish needed money to take the organisation forward, so he approached Hitesh Oberoi, his classmate from St. Columbus School and IIT-Delhi. Hitesh had known Yashish for over two decades and showed supreme confidence in his abilities. Hitesh understood the dynamics of the business well since he had been the MD and CEO of Info Edge, India's largest internet classifieds company that runs portals such as Naukri.com, Jeevansathi.com and 99acres.com, among others. He introduced Yashish to Sanjeev Bikhchandani, the founder of Info Edge. Coincidently, Sanjeev had taught at IIM-Ahmedabad when Yashish was a student there.

The first meeting was an eye-opener for Sanjeev. Yashish surprised him by telling him that he was paying 60 per cent more for his car insurance than he needed to. This statement intrigued Sanjeev, and he asked for a demo. Yashish demonstrated the prototype his team had built. The prototype substantiated Yashish's claim. There were cheaper policies available with similar features. Sanjeev felt that PolicyBazaar was solving a real problem. Trusting his instincts, he decided to back the team. Info Edge invested ₹20 crore and came on board as the first investor in the company. Yashish says, 'I feel a lot of gratitude towards Hitesh and Sanjeev for supporting us in those days when we were no one.'

Given the lack of investment advice for consumers, PolicyBazaar commenced its operations by showcasing the costs and features of various insurance plans. As it is difficult for established players to accept any change, initially insurers perceived PolicyBazaar as an enemy rather than a friend. None of them wanted to partner with PolicyBazaar. In the absence of support from insurers, the PolicyBazaar team analysed insurance products of various companies on their own and put them up on the website. This information helped in getting traffic from people looking for policies. Soon, thousands of policies were sold, and insurance companies started seeing the benefits of partnering with PolicyBazaar.

Earlier, consumers did not control what they were buying and agents often filled application forms with incorrect or misleading details. But PolicyBazaar came up with a strategy of asking around 80–90 questions to a potential buyer and considering features such as the buyer's age, occupation, health details, family history and lifestyle. This enabled the insurers to take informed decisions about who to sell policies to. Over time, insurers saw the merit in partnering with PolicyBazaar, and it became the largest aggregator and marketing channel for insurance companies.

PolicyBazaar's initial business model revolved around lead generation and advertisements. The company provided proper information to customers regarding insurance products. Based on their interest in the insurance product, it would pass on customer information to the insurance companies. By 2011, PolicyBazaar was working with 30 insurers and had reached a scale of ₹20 crores of annual revenue. Of this, 85 per cent came from lead generation and advertisements.

At that time, everything was moving in the right direction. PolicyBazaar had a great product, a brilliant team, fantastic technology, the right idea and a vast market. But no one could have foreseen how the future would pan out. In 2011, Insurance Regulatory and Development Authority (IRDA) came up with new regulations that put a cap on the money that web aggregators could charge insurers. Prior to this regulation, PolicyBazaar made ₹200 per lead, but later, this amount was restricted to a maximum of ₹10 per lead. Furthermore, PolicyBazaar would charge insurers for advertising their products on the portal. But the new regulation mandated that the aggregator couldn't charge insurers beyond ₹1 lakh per year for each displayed product. There were more rules for the renewal of the web aggregator licences, which were required every three years, and new rules for the mandatory training of employees. Unfortunately, the business became uneconomical, and PolicyBazaar went into a downward spiral.

Yashish says, 'The new rules were driven by multiple interests in the industry that aimed to maintain the status quo and saw PolicyBazaar as a threat. This was because PolicyBazaar wanted to explain and lay bare every product it sold, allowing the customer, for the first time, to make informed decisions.' The company struggled for the next three years, but Yashish and his team did not give up. When the world was predicting the slow death of PolicyBazaar, Yashish was planning a new business model to make things work. He saved the company by switching it from a lead-generation business to a platform that enabled financial transactions.

In the previous model, PolicyBazaar would generate leads for the insurers, who would transfer these leads to their call centres for conversion. PolicyBazaar would then get paid by the insurers for the leads that got converted. There was no uniformity in conversions, and leads would get wasted. The PolicyBazaar team proposed a new plan to the insurers. In this new plan they would handle insurance deals across the customer lifecycle from lead generation to running call centre operations, and from payment collection to policy issuance. Though a few insurers were prepared to give new work to PolicyBazaar, the company needed more funds to facilitate this transition. Yashish approached Sanjeev Bikhchandani for more funds. Sanjeev supported the business for two to three years. He invested just enough to convince new investors that the business had merit. Later on, many other investors came forward to invest in PolicyBazaar.

Jack Ma once said, 'Never give up. Today is hard, tomorrow will be worse, but the day after tomorrow will be sunshine.' By 2015, the regulations started changing, and the industry came around to Yashish's view that profitability lay in protection and not in investment. In other words, insurers started selling customers protection against disease, disability and death rather than offering complex investment products that also included insurance. As a result of simpler terms, the products became cheaper, making them more attractive to customers.

Though the situations were arduous, Yashish and his team persisted, and during this transformational journey, the company created many new business models and consumer-centric products. Now, over 100 million visitors come to PolicyBazaar annually for insurance advice, and over 10,00,000 policies are sold every month.

Focus on long-term value creation to attract customers

Value creation is what attracts customers to a brand; everything else is superficial. Yashish had always wondered why Indians were apprehensive of purchasing insurance despite it being affordable and beneficial. He learnt that there were many deterrents, such as complex product literature, the cumbersome buying process by mis-selling agents and an absence of assistance while making claims. Thus, he set about solving these problems and started putting the customer first.

PolicyBazaar started focusing on establishing and strengthening the digital channel of distribution, which was alien to customers. However, this new model had its own set of challenges. For customers to switch to a new channel for policy purchases, PolicyBazaar had to inspire trust within its clientele. During the transition, Yashish and his team realised that the biggest impediment to insurance growth was a lack of consumer-centric products in the market, especially in the death, disease and disability (three Ds) segments. Thus, the company's focus shifted from distribution to the creation of 'protection products' in the three Ds categories. PolicyBazaar focused on bringing free traffic to the website. Short ads that were informational as well as entertaining were created.

Since it started, PolicyBazaar has been educating people about comparing insurance products before buying them. It has always emphasised that people should not only compare premiums but also understand the benefits offered by various plans before finalising one. The root cause of the problem was a lack of jargon-free literature on the subject. In order to create trust, the company created an in-house PR team that focused on educating consumers through a content-led strategy. The team simplified insurance literature and started seeding media stories about insurance, its utility and product offerings. It used print, digital and audio-visual media effectively for this purpose. Moreover, it ran four television shows every week for consumer education on channels such as Headlines Today, Zee News, Zee Business and CNBC Awaaz. In these shows, the PolicyBazaar team talked about different products, how to make better decisions while buying insurance, identifying the insurance needs of people, finding the right product and so on.

While analysing the challenges faced by the Indian working class, Yashish also found that insurance as a product is sold and not bought. India has the lowest penetration of pure life insurance in the world. This is upsetting, especially considering our large population. The weight of personal calamities is hanging on the heads of more or less everyone, and there is no way such situations can be managed without insurance. With rising uncertainties that challenge our security every day, every family needs a life insurance cover that provides financial security in the absence of their breadwinner. However, each family's financial needs are different. To meet this increasing demand for variations in life insurance policies, PolicyBazaar has worked with insurers to come up with customised plans that cater to the varying needs of different individuals and families. By November 2019, PolicyBazaar accounted for 50 per cent of the market share among all online insurers and 90 per cent among aggregators. Furthermore, it had a 25 per cent market share in the life insurance segment.

Surprisingly, even health insurance cover in India is very low. Many workplaces in India have high-risk equipment, which makes for staggeringly high probabilities of death and fatal injuries. This, coupled with the rise of lifestyle and environmental diseases, makes it essential to invest in health insurance plans that can cover various aspects of unexpected hospitalisation. In the absence of suitable health insurance, the cost of medical treatment either eats into people's savings or people end up borrowing money. PolicyBazaar has created awareness about health insurance and has worked with insurers to come up with customised products. Over time, it has emerged as the largest distributor of health insurance policies in the country.

PolicyBazaar has always strived to provide customer satisfaction, and this has helped them achieve tremendous success. For instance, in the event of a motor insurance policy having lapsed, insurance companies insist on conducting a physical verification of the vehicle. Not only is this process inconvenient, it is also time-consuming as it takes anywhere between three to five days. To resolve this problem, PolicyBazaar developed a self-inspection video feature that allows customers to upload the documents required along with a video of the car. The uploaded information is shared instantly with the insurer without any human intervention, reducing the entire exercise to a matter of a few hours. Yashish says, 'With this innovation, we have essentially been able to kill two birds with one stone—we have resolved the issue of time and convenience for our consumers and reduced the costs involved for insurers.' Within three months of implementing this feature, PolicyBazaar recorded a 106 per cent growth in lapsed insurance policy revenue. Moreover, motor insurance conversions went up by about 51 per cent. Besides, there has been a reduction in the cost for insurers by ₹350 per acquired policy.

On the customer experience front, there have been several wins. Earlier, issuing a policy would take quite a while because, often, inspection did not happen on time. Moreover, trying to match the availability of an inspection team to the schedule of the customer added to the pain. These two issues would lead to a barrage of complaints by customers. Since the launch of the feature discussed earlier, consumer complaints regarding policy renewals have come down from an average of five complaints a day to one complaint a day.

Yashish says, 'Our vision is to make the 250 million-plus Indian households insurance aware and socially secured. We keep our heads down and go about doing what we do best—offer our customers a very high level of assisted and non-assisted support and services, personalised product offerings to suit their unique requirements, and a seamless buying experience.'

Use creative ways to connect with consumers

Insurance as an e-commerce business is very different from other e-commerce businesses like travel and retail. Unlike travel and retail, insurance is an information-heavy business, and unfortunately, people get bored while reading about it in detail. Also, while discounts are used liberally by online retail and travel businesses to attract users, this approach doesn't work in the insurance industry. Furthermore, travelling and shopping are mainly associated with fun, whereas buying insurance is associated with situations we would rather not think about.

Given the unattractiveness of the industry for consumers, it was not easy for PolicyBazaar to emotionally connect with its target audience. Moreover, since insurance remains a 'push' category dominated by agents and other distributors, the team realised that this was a battle of perceptions. The team used an intelligent mix of marketing and PR campaigns by using content that resonated with issues that the consumers faced. The uniqueness of this content was that it presented tedious and complicated topics in humorous and entertaining ways.

For instance, PolicyBazaar wanted to educate people about the need to compare insurance products before buying. The team wanted to encourage people to not only compare the premium but also understand what benefits each plan offered.

So, they launched a systematic campaign to cement the message that without comparing policies, one could be taken for a ride, which would ruin their savings. The company roped in comedian and TV personality Kapil Sharma as its brand ambassador. It launched a TV commercial, in which Kapil Sharma featured in different avatars and said '*Ab India Nahi Banega Ullu*'. Traditional channels such as TV, radio and outdoor advertising, which have the highest reach in the country, were used for this campaign. Kapil Sharma connected well with the audience and created awareness around PolicyBazaar's USP of giving customers the power to compare policies.

With the larger goal of building social security for households in India, PolicyBazaar launched a series of informative advertisements with a tagline, *'Taalo nahi, PolicyBazaar.com se le daalo'*. For this campaign series, the brand partnered with Bollywood actor Akshay Kumar, who appeared as Yamraj and educated people about the complications their families could face in the absence of a primary earner. For instance, one of the TV commercials starts in a hospital room where a dead man is lying on the bed, and Akshay Kumar dressed as Yamraj pays the dead man a visit to take him on his final pilgrimage. The patient shares with Kumar his predicament of having to leave his family in distress on account of unpaid EMIs, bills and other responsibilities such as his children's education and wedding expenses. At this juncture, Kumar prods him for not thinking about his family when he had the time to do so and reminds the audience that a term plan of ₹1 crore costs only ₹680 per month (for a 30-year-old non-smoker as of 14 November 2019). The brand has launched many similar advertisements with Akshay Kumar.

Medical inflation in India is increasing at an alarming rate. Unfortunately, the health insurance penetration in India is abysmally low, and roughly around 70 per cent of medical expenses are borne out of pocket by most Indians. To make customers realise the advantages of health insurance to safeguard against any unforeseen medical events, PolicyBazaar launched a health insurance campaign with actor Pankaj Tripathi. In the advertisement, Tripathi acts as a contractor trying to bribe an officer who has a sick husband. But the officer refuses the bribe and informs him that she does not need any money since she has a good health insurance policy that she got from PolicyBazaar.com. This advertisement reinforces its message at the end '*Majboori nahi, health insurance chuniye*'. On similar lines, PolicyBazaar has launched many humorous and informative advertisements that have created awareness about the benefits of getting a good insurance policy.

PolicyBazaar is a 'digital first' brand. It extensively uses digital media to interact with consumers across various buying stages, which are broadly divided into awareness, consideration and improved customer experience. Display ads, online PR, mobile app and active presence on social media can help any business increase the brand awareness in the digital space. Additionally, SEM, SEO, website reviews, blogs and reliable content take centre stage to convert brand awareness into lead generation. From a customer experience perspective, the brand reaches out to its target audience across social media platforms and attempts to solve their queries to ensure a seamless experience. At this stage, a lot of effort and resources are directed towards establishing and maintaining positive customer sentiment.

The fact that social media allows a brand to have a two-way dialogue with its audience makes it different from other marketing mediums. PolicyBazaar tries to leverage this unique advantage by building a community of active followers who not only engage with the brand online but also help the brand through their word-of-mouth advocacy.

Using active marketing communication, product customisation and a customer-centric approach, PolicyBazaar has been able to convince customers and partners to see insurance as a shield rather than something to be bought in order to save on tax. Inspiringly, the customer repeat rate for PolicyBazaar is 95 per cent against the industry average of 65 per cent. Furthermore, as a brand, PolicyBazaar has gained a lot of traction so much so that the company experienced faster growth when it expanded to the UAE. The UAE has a huge Indian diaspora, which was already aware of the brand and helped with word-of-mouth publicity amongst their non-Indian peers.

Embed constant innovation in the DNA of your business

Steve Jobs said, 'Innovation distinguishes between a leader and a follower.' Since its inception, PolicyBazaar's focus on innovation has not only helped it become a market leader but has also enabled it to sustain its leadership position in a highly competitive market.

Yashish divides insurance products into two broad categories: One, products dealing with highly important aspects of human life that require big decisions, such as health, life and disability. These products are purchased by customers primarily to create a safety net. There is no compulsion for customers to buy these products, and often advisers have to nudge customers to buy them. Two, products mandated by law, such as motor insurance and travel insurance. Customers cannot avoid these products. For selling the products mandated by law, the company doesn't need a push, and transactions happen through automation.

Insurance cannot be sold with a one-size-fits-all approach. Each customer is unique, and so are their requirements.

Therefore, segmentation and need identification are an integral part of business operations. Along with regular data analysis, the company also focuses on voice analytics. Calls are converted to text and analysed for words indicative of claims, fraud and miscommunication by agents. Analysing existing data helps PolicyBazaar unearth fraudulent claims by identifying words commonly used by customers who have made such claims earlier. Because of the analysis done by PolicyBazaar, insurers today have a fair idea of a potential customer's claim ratio, and it becomes easier to check whether or not the claim is genuine.

On any given day, PolicyBazaar advisers receive nearly 50,000 queries. To help out its advisers, PolicyBazaar introduced India's first artificial intelligence chatbot, PBee. Designed to provide professional, optimised and standardised customer support for all general queries, PBee also has the unique ability to provide insurance quotes after analysing a customer's requirements in detail. PBee has had a significant impact on the company's operational efficiency. It has reduced the response time from as long as 25–30 seconds to an instant response, resulting in higher output and customer satisfaction. The customer satisfaction ratings have increased from 60 per cent to 85 per cent. With better customer service, the brand image and position of the company has also gone up significantly.

In 2017, the number of average transactions grew from 1,20,000 to 2,50,000 within a month. This meant that the team was managing more consumers and solving more of their problems than ever before. In a nutshell, the team managed nearly 100 million customer queries over the phone. The company needed to innovate to keep up with this growth. To take its customer services to the next level, the company adopted Amazon Polly, a text-to-speech solution. Amazon Polly made a difference to the processes and efficiency by enabling the shift from sharing one-size-fits-all, predefined responses to personalised responses relevant to specific problems.

Later, the team integrated Amazon Polly with PBee and was able to increase its workforce productivity, decrease the time spent on customer handling, and substantially improve customer engagement, particularly for those calls where there is a specific call to action. PolicyBazaar now intends to build a voice bot, PBee Talk, that would use Amazon Polly for post-sales support. This will enable customers to speak to the company on its toll-free number and find answers to their queries. This will be achieved by integrating text-to-speech and speech-to-text features. The team envisions Amazon Polly to be a game-changer for its clients who might have literacy challenges or might be visually impaired.

Similarly, the company has focused on many other innovations. Yashish says, 'We do not believe in sitting on past laurels. Each day is a new day which comes with its own set of challenges, where we need to innovate.' With its focus on innovation, PolicyBazaar has been able to achieve 100 per cent year-on-year growth since its inception in 2008.

Staying healthy and generous plays a significant role in business growth

Yashish says, 'Fitness is essential for the overall growth of an individual. If you want to fare well as a professional, you need to be high on energy and have a positive attitude in life and towards your work. Sports teach you this and teach you to never give up. This attitude is crucial for the growth of an organisation.'

Yashish's day typically starts at 3.30 a.m. with his daily workout regime. He loves cycling, running and swimming. He can cycle for over 100 km and run over 50 km at a stretch. He also participated in one of the toughest endurance races in the world, known as the Iron Man Triathlon, in Sweden. It took him 11 hours and 39 minutes to finish the race, which included swimming 3.86 km, cycling 180 km and running 42 km. He also participated in two Delhi International Triathlons, one a sprint and the other a half-marathon, and won both across all age groups.

Yashish reaches the office before most people punch in. Being a CEO, his job is to meet people, handle issues and talk to investors. Although he has to take care of multiple things and has to switch gears numerous times a day, being a sportsperson, Yashish is always high on energy. He says, 'I feel the amount of hard work, dedication and perseverance that I have put in my sports, be it swimming or anything else, has taught me to be all the more dedicated to my company.' It is his fitness regime that has helped Yashish survive the downturns in business even when the regulator and insurance companies stood against his startup.

No wonder he loves to hire colleagues who are also athletes. According to Yashish, one can train employees for job requirements but not change their work ethics. He says, 'Employees who are athletes have strong optimism, commitment levels and dedication.' Staying fit and healthy plays a big role in sound and rational decision-making at work. To promote fitness, the company organises sports meets for its employees annually and encourages them to participate in different sporting events in and around the city. Apart from this, the company has fitness trainers on board to drive its employees to achieve their fitness and nutrition goals.

Although PolicyBazaar is one of the most funded startups in the country, Yashish likes to save cash just the way he likes to conserve energy for the final leg of a game. He says, 'Don't be in a rush to scale-up operations by burning cash because investors are not doing charity. If they have invested in your business, they are bound to expect returns. Remember that Rome was not built in a day. Our success can be attributed to the fact that we managed to earn back what we spend (daily).'

Yashish believes that distribution of wealth is vital for the creation of wealth. When Ebookers was acquired, the founders had made 2 million pounds, but Yashish could only manage 16,000 pounds. This was because he had never thought about having equity in the company. However, when he founded PolicyBazaar, he thought about his employees. PolicyBazaar is among the very few companies where management gets a bigger share than the founders: 65 per cent of the wealth is distributed to the management of the company and only 35 per cent is retained by the founders. Yashish says, 'The sole reason for the success of PolicyBazaar has been the people behind the scenes. So, the company gives a lot of weight to the people. They are our best resource and brand ambassadors.'

Besides this, Yashish likes to lead by example. He believes that is the only way to inspire confidence among employees. He believes in empowering the company's employees and giving them a freehand in accomplishing the task they have been entrusted with. He does not like to micromanage and believes in the ownership of work. He always backs an employee who has made an honest mistake because he believes that mistakes are made when one is working.

Within PolicyBazaar, many new ideas have been incubated, and a few of them have emerged as high-growth ventures. Incubated in 2014, PaisaBazaar is now India's largest online financial marketplace for loans and credit cards. Every year, more than 40 million people visit the PaisaBazaar website. PolicyBazaar also forayed into the health-tech space with Docprime, which commenced operations in 2018 and continues to grow. Many other ideas come from within the company, and new opportunities are constantly emerging for its employees. Yashish says, 'I want PolicyBazaar to be a brand where the top 50 people in the organisation operate 50 different business entities. So, while the success has been phenomenal, I would say we are just warming up to break new barriers.'

> Steve Jobs said, 'That's been one of my mantras—focus and simplicity. Simple can be harder than complex: You have to work hard to get your thinking clean to make it simple. But it's worth it in the end because once you get there, you can move mountains.' This mantra of focus and simplicity has also been the foundation of Yashish's entrepreneurial journey. It took a lot of focus for Yashish and his team to truly understand the underlying challenges in the insurance industry and come up with simplified solutions for customers. But eventually, they moved all the mountains and created one of the most popular internet brands in India.

YASHISH DAHIYA

Advice from Yashish Dahiya

- For a business to be successful, customer retention is crucial, and it takes precedence over customer acquisition. While marketing gives an initial push, organic traffic is the key to creating a sustainable brand, and it is cost-effective as well. So, always be aware of the real value you are providing to the customer.
- Observe your competitors, big or small. If they are doing anything sensible, then respond appropriately. If Yahoo had responded to Google when the search-engine ecosystem was evolving, Yahoo would not have been where it is now. At the same time, keep in mind that understanding your competition is good, but don't let it overwhelm you. At the end of the day, you have to bring something unique to the table.
- In business, you are going to face difficult situations at one point or another. But that doesn't mean you abandon the ship. Doing that is not an option. You lay low but keep going. See the bigger goal. Tweak the smaller ones. Do whatever it takes to sustain, but don't leave in between. Success only comes to those who don't stop. As the saying goes, the night is darkest just before dawn. Keep going strong even at the darkest hour.
- Finding the right person for the right job is crucial for your business. This is especially important for startups, as everything other than human resources can be managed.
- Always believe in yourself. You are going to win more often than lose by doing so.

Zoomcar
Never Stop Living

Creating a trend of subscription-based vehicle ownership in India

In America, Silicon Valley is considered home to many of the world's largest and most innovative technology companies, including Apple, Google and Facebook. The stories of Indians like Vinod Khosla and Sabeer Bhatia, who moved from India to Silicon Valley and founded companies like Sun Microsystems and Hotmail, are well known. But the stories of Americans who moved to India and made their mark have largely remained unheard of. The story of the American duo Greg Moran and David Back is one such example.

In 2012, Greg and David moved to Bengaluru, the Silicon Valley of India, and founded Zoomcar. Started in the year 2013 from one city with just seven cars, by July 2019 Zoomcar had expanded to over 47 cities with a fleet of over 11,000 cars. Moreover, more than 5 million customers had had the Zoomcar experience over 7 million times. Today, Zoomcar is India's largest self-drive mobility platform, which allows people to rent cars (without a chauffeur) by the hour, day, week and month. Through its managed marketplace model, Zoomcar is multiplying its fleet of cars and rapidly expanding its presence across India.

In its brief journey, Zoomcar has received many recognitions, including being called one of the top 10 most innovative companies from India by Fast Company. According to media reports, Zoomcar has received significant funding from many renowned investors, including Sequoia Capital, Nokia Growth Partners, Ford Motor Company, Mahindra & Mahindra, OurCrowd, FundersClub, Empire Angels, Trifecta Capital and other prominent angel investors such as Mohandas Pai.

This chapter covers the journey of Zoomcar, a brand that is redefining environment-friendly transportation in India.

THE BEGINNING

Born and raised in New York City, Greg attended the University of Pennsylvania to pursue a bachelor's degree in international relations with a focus on finance. There, he made friends with Indian students from Bengaluru, Mumbai, Delhi and Pune. Frequent and prolonged discussions about India with his friends and their families made India sound exciting to Greg. Additionally, he studied India academically as a part of his course. Through studies and conversations, he realised that America had hit a certain threshold, and its growth would not be the kind of growth that India could witness in the coming 20 to 30 years.

Because of his interest in the environment and sustainable development, after graduating in 2007, Greg joined an investment bank in New York City that focused on clean-tech and renewable energy. Interestingly, this firm had an office in Hyderabad. Some of the projects that his firm executed in India helped Greg identify the infrastructural gaps and lacunae in the Indian system that could potentially become significant business opportunities.

In 2011, Greg began discussing formal startup ideas for the Indian market with his friend from the University of Pennsylvania, David Back, who was pursuing his MBA at the Judge Business School at the University of Cambridge then.

The duo initially dabbled with the idea of starting a company in the renewable energy space, but when they realised that due to economic reasons and infrastructural limitations, car ownership would hit a wall in India, they zeroed in on the transportation sector. Though the global car rental space was buzzing with activity, in India, the car rental market was nascent. Cars were still booked through calls, and the process was unorganised and unstructured. At this time, Meru and Mega Cabs dominated the space, Uber was about to enter India and Ola was just coming into being. With no significant player focusing on this segment, the Indian market appeared to be a virgin territory and a billion-dollar opportunity.

In 2011, Greg decided to explore India and took an extended trip to the country before joining a business school in America. For three months, he travelled across 25 cities, including Bengaluru, Mangalore, Hyderabad, Mysore, Chennai, Ahmedabad, Surat, Delhi, Agra and Goa. He talked to thousands of people regarding their urban transport options. During this exploration phase, he realised that shared mobility could be a part of the future of Indian cities. At the end of the trip, Greg had a clear vision for the blueprint of Zoomcar.

As timing is everything, Greg did not want to delay the launch. He dropped out of business school, collected $1,00,000 from professional contacts and personal savings, and incorporated Zoomcar in a tiny office space near UB City, Bengaluru, in September 2012. After struggling for over five months, Zoomcar acquired the licence to run the business, and operations started in February 2013. By then, David had also dropped out of business school and joined the company in Bengaluru.

THE BRAND NAME: ZOOMCAR

If a brand name is catchy and can create a positive perception in the minds of customers, then it acts as a significant differentiating factor in a crowded market. But coming up with a brand name is not an easy process, and it requires a lot of iteration and validation.

Back in 2011, when Greg was discussing the business model of a self-drive car rental service with a few people, he created 'Your Car' as a placeholder for the brand name. To replace this placeholder with a proper brand name, he started discussing options with various groups and would come up with at least five names every day. Looking at the names of popular brands like Nike, Uber and Apple, he realised what worked for them—these names were short, clear and easy to remember. For his company, he wanted a name that had these attributes and also sounded trustworthy. Moreover, since his target market was India, he wanted the brand name to play well with Indian languages.

The word 'zoom' means to move very rapidly and sounds like a car speeding by on a road. Interestingly, in the Indian context, there are not many brand names that start with the letter 'Z', so this name was distinct and showed a potential to stand out. The word also ticked all the boxes that Greg had in mind for the brand name. The brand thus came to be named Zoomcar.

BUSINESS LESSONS

Many important business lessons can be learnt from the evolution of Zoomcar.

Look for a market-creation opportunity over a market-sharing opportunity

Blue Ocean Strategy is a classic book that explains the terms 'red ocean' and 'blue ocean' that are often used to describe a market. Red oceans are established markets in which companies try to outperform their competitors to grab a share of existing demand. As the market space gets crowded, products become commodities, and profit and growth reduce. On the other hand, blue oceans are unexplored and uncontested markets, in which competition is insignificant, and demand is created rather than fought for.

In developed markets like the USA, the self-drive car rental space is crowded with established players like the Avis Budget Group, Enterprise Rent-A-Car, Turo, Silvercar, Zipcar and others. Any new player in this market will have to face intense competition to gain market share. In a way, this market is a red ocean. In contrast, when Greg and David planned to start Zoomcar, the Indian car rental market was unexplored territory. It was predominantly offline and dominated by a few unorganised legacy businesses. Moreover, ownership of vehicles is a massive hassle in India due to issues like cost, traffic, lack of parking spaces, insurance and maintenance charges, etc. So, this market seemed like a blue ocean with enormous potential.

As blue ocean markets are new, the market creator has to go through numerous challenges to organise things and educate the market. Unlike software businesses, transportation businesses are not easy to start in India. To set up a car rental business in India, Zoomcar needed a licence which, initially, they were unable to acquire due to regulatory issues. Between September 2012 and December 2012, Greg unsuccessfully ran from pillar to post to secure a licence. The only way out was to work with an existing player who already had a one. At that point in time, there were five such players in India, but four of them rejected Greg's request.

Dale Carnegie said, 'Most of the important things in the world have been accomplished by people who have kept on trying when there seemed to be no hope at all.' Following such a philosophy, even after many unsuccessful attempts, Greg kept on trying. In the first week of December 2012, a meeting with Ford Motors in Delhi led Greg to a Bengaluru-based car dealer, who in turn connected Greg with Ramesh Tours and Travels, the fifth player in India with the required licence. Greg had one final meeting with Ramesh Tours and Travels on 23 December 2012. If this meeting hadn't gone his way, Greg might have moved back to America. Fortunately, Ramesh Tours and Travels agreed to the terms and worked out a licencing agreement with Greg.

On 14 February 2013, Zoomcar kicked off business in Bengaluru with four Ford Figos and three Mahindra Scorpios. The company allowed customers to book rides, make payments, and board cars that were stationed across multiple locations in the city.

As Zoomcar was managing its own fleet of cars, it was a capital-intensive business. To scale-up the business, the company needed more cars, and to roll out more cars, they needed more money. Greg reached out to many investors in India, but they were not interested in the concept. The investors saw this to be a tough business model in terms of execution risk. Moreover, they were unsure whether the American duo would continue to run the business in India.

As the duo didn't get a favourable response from investors in India, they decided to try their luck with their connections in America. Between his graduation and MBA admission, David had pursued a law degree at Harvard Law School, where he had been a teaching assistant to Larry Summers, the former US Treasury Secretary and professor at Harvard University. Fortunately, Summers agreed to invest in the company as an angel investor. As Zoomcar raised funds from Summers, *The Wall Street Journal* covered the company, and in the next five days, the duo received calls from five US-based angel investors. All five ended up investing, and this investment helped Zoomcar scale its fleet up to 50 cars in Bengaluru.

Investors in India were still not taking Zoomcar seriously. To scale-up further, the duo raised another million dollars from a few marquee investors in New York and San Francisco, including, among others, the former commissioner of the US Securities and Exchanges, Lady Barbara Judge. In March 2014, Zoomcar further raised $1.5 million from existing investors and some angel investors from Dubai. This money gave the company the firepower to branch out to Pune with 25 vehicles. A multi-city presence helped in winning the confidence of investors in India. In October 2014, Sequoia Capital, former Infosys chief financial officer (CFO) T.V. Mohandas Pai, and a few others pumped $8 million into the company. With this funding, Zoomcar launched its operations in Delhi, followed by Mumbai, Chennai and Hyderabad.

Meanwhile, for market creation, Zoomcar targeted an upwardly mobile and young audience who come to a new city to work or study. Car ownership can be a significant drain given the initial cost of the vehicle—leasing, financing, insurance, parking, fuel, taxes and other expenses. In fact, even people who owned small cars started renting bigger cars for vacation. To provide a better experience to its customers, Zoomcar started delivering cars to customers' doorsteps for a nominal fee. This home delivery service was an innovation, which lead to a 20 per cent increase in adoptions within a week.

To scale faster in new markets and meet demands within existing markets, Zoomcar needed more cars. Owning a fleet of cars meant incurring huge costs, and their maintenance was impacting profits. Rather than self-owned cars, the company decided to bring more cars from non-bank sources. In 2016, the company launched a programme to source vehicles from third-party operators and from individuals with a high net worth. The company's growth proved too robust for even this supply model. In early 2018, Zoomcar launched a shared subscription service, which allowed customers to borrow a car for a fixed tenure of six to 36 months without the hassles of down payment, car loan and maintenance or insurance cost. In turn, this programme allowed the subscribers to 'share back' the vehicle with Zoomcar when not used in a personal capacity. This created a substantially more affordable way for individuals to access a personal car.

To increase its presence in new states, the company is in talks with various state governments to solve the regulatory issues surrounding a commercial licence for a private car. Aping the Zoomcar growth story, many new players have forayed into the market. However, Zoomcar holds the distinction of being the country's first self-drive car rental company, which created the market in India.

Think outside the box to get inside customers' heads

In today's market, which is quite crowded, creating brand awareness becomes a herculean task, which is further complicated by the ever-decreasing attention span of customers. So Zoomcar had to stand out. Being a startup with a lot of investments made on cars and the team, money was a limitation for Zoomcar. So, Greg looked for unpaid and low-cost ways of marketing. To add virality into the product itself, cars with bright colours like red, green, orange and blue were included in the fleet. These cars stood out and Zoomcar's branding on them helped create brand awareness.

As a matter of fact, when Zoomcar started, car vendors would charge an absurd amount of deposit money while giving a car on rent. That one could rent a car with a refundable deposit of only ₹5,000 was unthinkable. This small deposit amount encouraged people to rent cars and added to the popularity of the brand. To reach out to the young working crowd, the team partnered with companies like Amazon and parked cars at noticeable spots in parking spaces. Companies spoke about the service to their employees, and the loud colours of the cars attracted them. Similarly, to reach out to college students, Zoomcar sponsored college events by providing one or two cars. Moreover, the team distributed ride coupons at places where youngsters hung out, such as Café Coffee Day outlets.

To accelerate awareness, the team planned multiple roadshows around popular occasions. For instance, around Friendship Day, they replicated a car from the movie *Dumb and Dumber*. This car looked like a dog and was named the K9 Cruiser. The motto was that when everybody would be celebrating Friendship Day, Zoomcar would pay tribute to a person's best friend. This car was taken around many cities like Bengaluru, Mumbai, Pune, Hyderabad, Coimbatore and Chennai. Similarly, for Ganesh Chaturthi, the team created a car that looked like a mouse and was called Mushak.

The team even listed a horse named Dhanno along with their range of cars available for rent. Around the same time, they wrote blogs about why a horse is better than a car. Similarly, the team listed an auto on the platform with the message 'You've never driven an auto? You can rent one from Zoomcar and drive it.' One constant thing about the Zoomcar team is that it conducts innovative experiments to grow the brand by word of mouth.

After raising some funds, the company scaled its marketing investments to achieve targeted growth. Around 2015, the team launched a YouTube music video that conveyed the whole idea of Zoomcar through a musical number. This video focused on the theme of 'the freedom to drive on your own' and conveyed the story of a group of friends who use Zoomcar for their trip. This video became viral and helped the brand connect with people.

To engage with its target audience, the company has organised various on-ground events. For instance, a treasure hunt was organised in Hyderabad. Then, the company hosted a day-long musical getaway, Zoomapalooza, on the outskirts of Bengaluru to build top-of-the-mind recall with its core customers, who are typically college students and young professionals. To popularise this event, Zoomcar launched its marketing campaign across different media, including print, radio, outdoor and digital campaigns on social media channels, and engaged with music, travel and lifestyle bloggers.

As the young urban audience engages more with online activity rather than with TV programmes and ads, Zoomcar partnered with digital channel Filter Copy for a web series, *What the Folks*. Another online video *If Salary Were a Person* successfully clocked a whopping 25 million organic views. Within days of this video's debut on social media platforms, the ZAP subscriptions increased by 40 per cent. To reach the masses, the company launched a campaign for ZAP Subscribe, which was spread across TV, print, outdoor and online formats. As a result of this campaign, the number of subscriptions increased a hundred times. Furthermore, Zoomcar partnered with global call-identification service Truecaller to capitalise on the platform's 100 million daily active premium smartphone users in India. Through Truecaller, Zoomcar managed to achieve over 400 million impressions for its brand campaign, followed by user interest that led to direct conversions.

Because of its effective and innovative marketing strategies, Zoomcar has been able to gain significant mindshare and over 70 per cent of the market share.

Transform business processes through technology

Technology makes a business agile enough, delivers sustainable growth, and brings better customer experience. For Zoomcar, technology is a strategy for perpetual innovation across the past, present and future elements of the car rental business. Let us take a look at a few of these innovations.

While giving a car on rent, the biggest issue for a car vendor is the safety of his car. To verify drivers, Zoomcar has partnered with an identity verification provider—Onfido. Using a smartphone, Zoomcar users can upload a selfie and a photo of their identity document to complete the verification process. Through its machine learning and biometrics-based fraud detection, Onfido can check that the right person is getting the car keys. Moreover, the team can track cars in real-time using GPS technology and can take control of the car remotely through engine immobilisers installed in the cars.

Furthermore, when the market was unorganised, there were chances of people hiding their identity by paying in cash. To avoid any misuse of cars, from day one, Zoomcar only accepts payment digitally. As all digital payment options take care of customer KYC, in case of any issues, the company can trace the customer through their identity with the bank. Over time, Zoomcar has done several experiments to make its customer verification process robust. For example, since Aadhaar has become mandatory, the company has piloted Aadhaar checks.

As India has multiple languages, to avoid any translation error, Zoomcar does not take bookings on the phone. It has a digital interface for car bookings supported by a real-time car availability system at the backend. Also, earlier customers used to interact with field executives while renting and returning cars, but now, Zoomcar has automated this process through a digital checklist. Now, information is captured digitally, and any possible translation or communication errors are avoided.

To track demand, booking patterns, car locations within cities and other parameters, the team has created an admin panel that provides consistent information to every employee within the company. To avoid incidences of booking cancellations due to bad condition of cars, the team has created a monitoring system that notifies the field staff about investigating possible issues in case bookings are cancelled.

To avoid dependency on people for delivering keys, the company has devised a Key Less Entry (KLE) technology. Using this technology, a customer can lock and unlock their car through their smartphone, and if they want to loan their car to a friend or rent it to a paying stranger, they can send an access code to their phone. To make sure that KLE works properly in low network areas such as basements, the phone connects to the car via GPRS and Bluetooth.

To transform its strong fleet of cars into Internet of Things (IoT) enabled vehicles, Zoomcar launched Cadabra, an in-house software-cum-hardware platform. Equipped with Bluetooth and 4G cellular connectivity, Cadabra tracks over 100 signals, including real-time vehicle location, fuel levels, distance travelled, clutch position, harsh braking, inconsistent acceleration, seat belt usage and engine health, among others. If a car is prone to an accident due to rash driving, then Cadabra sends voice notifications to the driver. In the event of an accident, Cadabra can also connect with emergency services.

As Cadabra is a machine learning-based system, the more data Zoomcar's ecosystem generates, the more accurate and responsive Cadabra becomes. With Cadabra's intelligence, Zoomcar aims to reduce maintenance and servicing costs while allowing individuals to avoid accidents. Cadabra is fully integrated into the Zoomcar app and allows customers to review and rate trips, and keep track of the cumulative driver score. Also, it gives tips to improve driving behaviour (in real-time and post the trip).

As Zoomcar is scaling up, it is using high-end technology to streamline processes and improve customer safety and experience.

Make yourself and your team more productive

One of the pioneers of the self-improvement industry, Paul J. Meyer said, 'Productivity is never an accident. It is always the result of a commitment to excellence, intelligent planning, and focused effort.' At Zoomcar, Greg focuses on making himself and his team more productive so that they can make a significant impact through respective roles.

At every stage of the business, there are new sets of challenges, and Greg faces them with his resilience, perseverance and tenacity. More than anything else, his fitness programme helps him develop these skills. Fitness has been an integral part of Greg's life. While growing up in New York, he played tennis, basketball, American football and golf. He says, 'Playing a sport gives you a well-rounded personality.' Even though Greg works for over a hundred hours a week, he starts his day at 5.30 a.m. and runs about 10 km. Since 2013, when he began Zoomcar, he also began a CrossFit regime, a high-intensity fitness programme that incorporates elements from several sports and various types of exercises.

A corporate leader needs to have a patient and balanced approach towards their team and goals. As good cooking requires patience and balance of flavours and ingredients, Greg cooks a lot of healthy Indian, Thai and Italian food using superfoods like spinach, kale, sprouts, beetroot and sweet potatoes. He believes one needs more pursuits to live a holistic life. Other than a proper fitness regimen and an interest in cooking, he enjoys music and plays the piano. He believes it is crucial to have the support of family and friends, so he manages to go home to New York once or twice a year.

Greg thinks a leader should have a top-down vision in terms of where he wants to take his business in three to four years. But when he is building a core chain of customer experience, he has to look bottom-up and empathise with customers at every point. During the initial days of Zoomcar, Greg played every role within the company—from a call centre executive to a field representative to a car cleaner. Working in these roles helped him understand the nitty-gritties of his business. Similarly, he encourages his team to experience different aspects of the business. Moreover, for the holistic development of its employees, the company frequently organises sporting activities and training programmes.

According to Greg, the best business results come through collaboration, and within the organisation, collaboration happens when co-workers, teams and business functions empathise with each other. Zoomcar promotes the culture of cross-training so that employees in one function are well aware of the work of different functions. By getting a holistic perspective of the business, employees are able to link their objectives to the company's broader mission and collaborate well with other teams.

Growth in the front end takes a lot of effort in the back end

American singer and songwriter Frank Ocean, said, 'Work hard in silence, let your success be your noise.' With this spirit in mind, the Zoomcar team puts in a lot of effort in the back end to achieve growth and customer love. Today, Zoomcar is the largest and fastest-growing self-drive car service brand in India, but its journey evolved city by city, car by car, customer by customer, employee by employee, and innovation by innovation with numerous trials and errors.

To start with, Greg chose Bengaluru as the first market for Zoomcar. Being a technology and education hub, the city attracts many young people who migrate from different parts of India to work and study. These expats want to drive a car but don't have the money to make down payments. So, they prefer to rent rather than buy. Moreover, Bengaluru has lovely weather and there are many places close to the city where one can explore nature. To sum up, Bengaluru was a perfect market for Zoomcar to start.

Since its inception, customer experience has remained the company's top priority. One fundamental part of delivering a consistent experience to customers is the ability to provide a car that is in the best shape possible to every single customer. With that in mind, the company first focused on building the supply and distribution network and then marketed its services to create demand. For over 18 months, the team focused on building stable and scalable on-ground operations in Bengaluru.

After deploying 150 cars and achieving proven stability and operational efficiency in its first city, Zoomcar planned for its next stage of growth.

Choosing Pune as the second city was also a well-thought-out decision. As with Bengaluru, Pune has pleasant weather and many nearby places to explore natural beauty. Known as the Oxford of the East, the city of Pune has a huge student crowd. Moreover, because of the presence of big IT companies, Pune is considered one of the largest IT hubs in India. After stabilising operations in Pune, which took around six months, Zoomcar expanded its presence to Delhi NCR, then to Mumbai, and followed it up with Chennai, Hyderabad and Chandigarh. Before expanding into any more cities, the team spent around 15 months in stabilising their business operations across these cities.

The self-drive car rental business is about offering a hyper-local, neighbourhood-based service that is conveniently accessible to the community so that people can have access to a car any time anywhere. To provide superior customer experience, a granular understanding of users is critical. By analysing data on usage patterns, the company found different use cases for its services in different cities. For example, in a city like Bengaluru, locals hire cars for short vacations over the weekend and travellers hire cars on weekdays to get into town from the airport. Often, students hire cars in the night to ride in groups. As Zoomcar operates in different cities with varied use cases, it has to customise at least 20 per cent of its services as per each city's requirement. In every city, the company has created localised teams that understand the local culture, and ensure that cars are clean, in perfect working condition and available on time.

As the educational background of its field staff may not match that of its customers, Zoomcar focuses on grooming, training and empathy-building of its field staff. Empowering them with additional skills helps in boosting their morale, and they engage better with customers. To make sure that people working in the Zoomcar offices develop an understanding of the field operations, employees, including product managers and designers, work at a pickup site for a day, meet customers, observe the pickup process, and look for ways to improve it. They also work in the customer experience centre to hear what customers really think about the service. Sometimes they rent a Zoomcar and even competitors' cars to compare the experience. Through such initiatives, the company ensures that all its employees understand customer pain points and get back into a room to discuss how to build a seamless experience.

As business started evolving and scaling, it became necessary for the company to measure the right metrics for progress. Greg says, 'Entrepreneurs often chase vanity metrics they have heard somewhere or read in the media. That's a wrong approach. One should focus on metrics that matter for his business.' For Zoomcar, customer happiness and profitability are the two guiding principles. By keeping a balance between these principles, the company measures usage patterns, economics, frequency, engagement and other factors at the user, city, region and company levels. Using mathematical models to estimate demand, the team analyses usage trends on regular bookings. The team also analyses global car-rental trends as well as cost and pricing and other relevant metrics against alternative travel options.

The Zoomcar team is continuously striving to make its customers' rental experience effortless and delightful. In a short period, Zoomcar has become a brand that resonates with people who use rented cars to feed their love of travelling and exploring new places. The number of selfies and the amount of user-generated content around the brand on social media showcases how loved Zoomcar is among its customers.

In today's digital age, the conventional wisdom of owning an automobile for mobility no longer works. Instead, consumers are paying to access someone else's asset for a particular period. At the same time, for car owners, a private automobile that sits idle most of the time is an expensive proposition. By becoming an intermediary between car owners and consumers who don't know each other, Zoomcar is not only facilitating economic exchange, cost savings and convenience but also enabling environmental benefits on a large scale.

Greg says, 'We believe India is just the beginning for us. What we are building is very relevant and very contextual for markets such as Southeast Asia, Africa and other emerging economies.' In the future, it would be interesting to see the journey of Zoomcar from India to other countries.

Advice from Greg Moran

- In business schools, students focus on quantitative subjects and sometimes take subjects around organisational behaviour, negotiations and people dynamics lightly. In the business world, working with numbers helps up to a certain extent, but in the long run, understanding of organisational behaviour, people dynamics and negotiation skills distinguish a successful leader from others. Quantitative skills can always be better honed on the job than in the classroom.
- All great founders have to be great communicators because they have to communicate their vision and mission consistently. Furthermore, they have to be empathetic to manage stakeholders at multiple levels.

GREG MORAN

- The relation between failure and success is not binary. Failure doesn't mean 0, and success doesn't mean 1. The relationship between success and failure is relative, which means that during the process of trying something, a person might achieve several small successes 0.1, 0.2, 0.3 ... but if a few final steps don't work out, the overall outcome would not be the expected success (1). The small successes (0.1, 0.2, 0.3) achieved during the process should motivate a person to try one more time.

JOSH TALKS

Transforming India by empowering the youth

India has one of the youngest populations in the world, and the youth of the country is filled with talent and enthusiasm to achieve big things. If they get the right guidance, then in the coming years, India's youth can contribute immensely to the country's economic and social progress, and India can outshine the rest of the world. But the sad truth is, due to lack of exposure, a large section of the youth misses out on opportunities to do something meaningful with their lives.

Walt Disney said, 'If you can visualize it, if you can dream it, there's some way to do it.' Since many youngsters can't visualise the umpteen opportunities available and don't dream big, they waste their potential on unnecessary things such as addictive distractions, negative thinking, anti-social and destructive activities and so on. To expose the youth to innumerable possibilities, they need to be introduced to role models who have achieved their dreams by overcoming significant obstacles. And to turn this inspiration into action, the youth needs to be informed about the steps required to achieve their goals. Josh Talks has taken up this monumental task.

Josh Talks provides exposure to the youth by showcasing inspirational stories, giving career mentorship and developing skills through on-ground training. It produces online motivational videos through which achievers in various fields, including entrepreneurship, sports, stand-up comedy, social activism, public policy and performing arts, share their inspiring journeys. By May 2019, Josh Talks had covered over 1,500 speakers across nine languages: English, Hindi, Marathi, Bengali, Tamil, Punjabi, Gujarati, Malayalam and Telugu. Its YouTube channels have over 3 million subscribers, with over 30 million views monthly. The brand has a huge following on several social media channels, including more than 1 million subscribers on Facebook. Josh Talks also organises offline conferences and skill-building workshops. By May 2019, it had reached out to over 1,50,000 people offline through its events in 30 different cities and workshops in over 1,000 colleges.

Founded in January 2015 by two twenty-year-olds, Shobhit Banga and Supriya Paul, Josh Talks is one of India's largest and fastest-growing impact platforms. During its journey, the company has received numerous awards and recognitions, including the National Media Award by the erstwhile President of India Shri Ram Nath Kovind, Asia 30 Under 30 by *Forbes* magazine and Top 50 Startups of India by *The Economic Times*.

This chapter covers the inspiring journey of Josh Talks, a brand on a mission to create an ecosystem that can aid young people on their journey from where they are to where they want to be.

THE BEGINNING

Supriya Paul grew up in Gurgaon. She always focused on her academics. She wanted to grow up to be a doctor, as it was her dream to be able to cure diseases such as cancer. After clearing her Class X examinations, she took up science, but within two months she realised that it was not her cup of tea. She then decided to become an engineer and joined an IIT coaching class. However, soon she realised that engineering entrance preparation was a different kind of pressure, and she couldn't take it. Supriya convinced her parents and moved from science to the commerce stream. She enjoyed her subjects, secured a score of 96 per cent in her Class XII examinations, and joined Sri Venkateshwara College to pursue a BCom degree. She was thinking of becoming a chartered accountant (CA), as was almost everyone in her class. After her first exam though, she regretted her decision to pursue the profession. Unable to figure out her true calling, Supriya was not feeling good.

Supriya's father, a topper from the prestigious Shri Ram College of Commerce (SRCC), was very disappointed by her decision of giving up sought-after career options. For a period, Supriya went into a slump and wanted to know how people her age decide what they want to do and who they want to become. She found that most of them didn't make decisions based on passion but based on what others told them to do.

Unlike Supriya, Shobhit Banga grew up in Mandi, a small town in Himachal Pradesh. Due to his love for cycling, at the age of 15, he left conventional schooling and moved to Bengaluru to become a world-class cyclist. He lived in the servant's quarter of the house of a government official and started training to achieve his dream. At the age of 16, he became the youngest person to qualify for Paris–Brest–Paris, one of the most prestigious cycling events in the world. He then went on to become the youngest member of India's first professional cycling team.

In 2013, Shobhit moved to Delhi to pursue a bachelor's degree at GD Goenka World Institute. He was used to working 10–15 hours a day for building a dignified life of dreams and achievements. But he found that his peers in college were not motivated and had no clue about what they wanted to do with their lives. Even in other colleges, he found that many students were wasting their time and not attending classes regularly for a variety of reasons, such as elections, unavailability of teachers, or simply to spend time in the canteen or go for movies. He felt it was high time to give them a wake-up call so that they could utilise their potential and do something meaningful with their lives.

As luck would have it, Supriya met Shobhit at a party and happened to talk about the lack of motivational messaging and role models for the youth of the country. They exchanged their frustration over the fact that youngsters across India did not tap into their true potential and discussed ways to bring a change in the mindeset of the student community, broaden their horizons and shake things up. They talked about this for several months. Eventually, they decided to create a platform that would showcase the stories of people who had followed their passion and surpassed challenges and obstacles to achieve success. They felt that these stories could ignite a spark among students, young professionals and people from different walks of life. In 2014, the journey of Josh Talks started with a small event in Delhi.

THE BRAND NAME: JOSH TALKS

The team was looking for a name that would resonate with the masses and would inspire them. The Hindi word 'josh' means passion. It implies a boost to the thought process that can change the way people live their lives.

Both Shobhit and Supriya felt that to achieve their goals and overcome challenges, people need josh day in and day out. Moreover, the word 'josh' has a good recall value, so the brand name Josh Talks appeared to be a perfect fit.

While in college, Supriya and Shobhit organised an event on 6 April 2014 at the Air Force Auditorium in Dhaula Kuan, Delhi. Twelve speakers from varied backgrounds spoke at the event, and around 300 audience members between the ages of 16 and 21 showed up. The unique thing about this event was that instead of lecturing the youth about what they should do with their lives or talking about the future, speakers shared their stories of struggles and achievements. Even three months after the event, the team kept receiving inquiries about the next scheduled event.

This enthusiasm of the audience spurred the team's josh, and they decided to organise a few more college events. In December 2014, the team organised a large conference at SRCC. Bollywood actor Boman Irani, Goonj founder Anshu Gupta and the first female amputee in the world to climb Mount Everest Arunima Sinha were among the speakers. Over 6,000 people turned up. After this event, many people wrote to the team about the positive impact these talks had on their thought process. Looking at the success of the pilot events of 2014, in January 2015, the team launched Josh Talks officially.

BUSINESS LESSONS

Many important business lessons can be learnt from the evolution of Josh Talks.

Validate your product with customer feedback

Every new opportunity begins with a few years of trial and error, but by continually validating and evolving the product based on customer feedback, entrepreneurs can find their product-market fit. In 2015, Josh Talks organised eight events in Delhi, Bengaluru and Mumbai. To make these conferences accessible, the team either allowed free entry or charged nominal amounts. At the end of the year, the team realised that the impact of offline events was limited to the audiences who attended the events. To spread the word faster and further to people who didn't attend the events, especially the people in tier-2 and tier-3 cities, the team decided to move online and start an English language YouTube channel. The decision to move online changed the positioning of Josh Talks from a conference company to a media company. For six months, the company's basic offering was an English YouTube channel with talks similar to TEDx, INK and TiE.

While showing a few TED videos to kids at a few orphanages in Delhi, Shobhit realised that the English language was a barrier. Moreover, their target audience could not comprehend the topics covered, as the problems that an Indian audience, especially the poor or those from the middle class, face on a day-to-day basis are different. For example, a village boy will relate better with becoming a government officer or opening a small business than becoming a NASA scientist. Also, they would find it hard to connect with someone like Steve Jobs. Shobhit and Supriya found that if someone was to share their struggle (mental, financial or other) and the actions they undertook to overcome these struggles to reach where they are now, it would motivate the viewers to change their lives. Unfortunately, there was nobody catering extensively to the needs of this strata of the Indian audience.

The team wanted to create the content that their audience wanted. As the target audience of Josh Talks includes college students and young professionals, between the ages of 16 and 30 years, in tier-2, tier-3 and tier-4 cities, the team decided to change the language of the talks from English to Hinglish and Hindi. Furthermore, to create talks on topics that would be relatable to their target audience, the team did extensive research. They collected inputs from college students, analysed what kind of keywords their target audiences were searching on the internet, and what they were commenting on social media channels.

Based on their research, the team created their content strategy and defined popular buckets such as personality development, English speaking, government jobs and micro-entrepreneurships like opening a medical store. The team identified relatable role models catering to different buckets and approached them for talks. Over time, the team observed that most of the audience in small towns understood regional languages. To cater to the needs of audiences that prefer regional languages, multiple regional language channels were launched.

After looking at a few cases, the team realised that information on the internet was incomplete, and that the youth didn't just need inspiration but also information that could inspire action. For example, through her mother, Supriya met a village boy who used to work as a domestic help. In the course of her interaction with him, she found that the boy wanted a bank job because he thought it would allow him to live in his village, close to his family. He was not aware that a bank job could send him to other cities. The Josh Talks team conducted some research in and around his village and found that there were hardly any medical stores in that area. When they asked him if he would be interested in opening up a medical store in his village, he showed great interest. The team guided him through the steps required to open a medical store including how to get a bank loan. With their guidance, the boy was able to shift his focus in a direction that would serve his purpose.

Another instance was when the team, while going through the comments on one of the videos posted by Josh Talks, got to know about a boy who despite years of hard work couldn't get into the Army because of a tattoo on his body. Unfortunately, he didn't understand English and had not understood the clause related to tattoos. To help these kinds of cases, the team started Josh Kosh, a career guidance platform with intense modules on how to start a business or get into a particular type of job. The team is putting together a skill curriculum that can help students get a job or become business-ready. They are also working on making a database of opportunities available, organised by pin codes. Thus, based on user feedback, the team continuously works on new solutions that can make a bigger and better impact.

Even small can make a big impact

In the dictionary, we find different synonyms for the word small such as young, limited in number, not outstanding, of little importance and so on. By looking at these meanings, sometimes, we devalue the power of small. But when small efforts are aggregated, they have the power to make a significant impact. For example, Dashrath Manjhi, also known as Mountain Man, was a labourer in the village of Gehlaur in Bihar. Using only a hammer and chisel, he carved a path 110 m long, 9.1 m wide and 7.6 m deep through a hillock. Because of his 22 years of work, travel between the Atri and Wazirganj blocks of Gaya (a town in Bihar) was shortened from 55 km to 15 km.

If we look at the Josh Talks team, everyone is at the threshold of adulthood, being under 25 years of age. If we look at Josh Talks videos, they are of a small duration of 12–15 minutes. If we look at the frequency of video uploads, only two videos per regional channel are uploaded every week. If we look at the speakers, most of them come from small towns. The same holds for its audience. But if we look at the impact, it is huge. In the short span of a few years, Josh Talks has covered over 1,500 speakers in nine languages, and its YouTube channels have over 3 million subscribers with over 30 million views monthly.

Along with audiences, Josh Talks has also made an impact on the lives of many of its speakers. For example, through Amazon seller success stories, the team got to know about Bimal Majumdar, a small leather products seller from Kolkata. Bimal came from a very poor family. In 1992, after an argument with his parents, he shifted to Kolkata with only ₹37 in his pocket. While working as a security guard, he learnt how to make pure leather products. After that, he worked for about four or five more companies. While learning and working, he also started his business on the side and eventually became a popular seller on Amazon. His Josh Talk became the first talk to hit a million views on the Bengali channel. After the talk, he got invited as a special speaker to multiple events and became one of Amazon's famous success stories. A lot of business people from Kolkata reached out to him to establish business relations with him.

Similarly, the Josh Talks team came across Amruta Soni, a transgender government employee. They tried finding her contact details but were unable to do so. They reached out to the NGO listed in the article and, through them, were eventually able to connect with her. Amruta was raped at the age of 16 and pushed into sex work, but she fought even in her darkest hours and became a government official. Her Josh Talk video has over 5 million views, and she has also spoken at the UN Women event organised in partnership with Josh Talks. Interestingly, seeing the popularity of her video, a college that earlier had denied her admission called her for a session.

To bring about social change, Josh Talks has worked on campaigns like Citizen Townhall. India is the world's largest democracy, but the first-time voter turnout is meagre. During the 2019 elections, to increase awareness among citizens, including over 130 million first-time voters about the civic responsibility to vote, Josh Talks, in partnership with Facebook, organised a Citizen Townhall. The objective of this multi-city initiative was to empower youth with the knowledge they needed to participate in the elections effectively. Events were organised across 15 states and senior government officials of the states, including chief electoral officers, and voting activists participated in discussions with the youth and answered their questions. Also, Josh Talks brought forward stories of people who did interesting stuff to motivate others to vote. For example, in Karnataka, a family had a wedding card designed like voter IDs. Similarly, many other interesting stories were shared.

There is a famous dialogue in the movie Manjhi—'*Bhagwan ke bharose mat baithiye, kya pata Bhagwan humre bharose baitha ho!*' Instead of waiting for some big organisation to bring changes, the team at Josh Talks is trying to bring significant changes through their small but continuous efforts.

Don't postpone monetisation and profitability

Revenue generation is essential to building a company, but many startups delay monetisation for too long and depend on venture capital till they create a self-sustaining business. Sadly, if they are not able to raise capital when needed, they have to slow down or shut down the business.

Josh Talks witnessed losses of ₹10 lakhs and ₹50 lakhs in 2015 and 2016, respectively. But through its monetisation techniques, it broke even in 2017. Interestingly, the company made a profit of around ₹75 lakhs in 2018. Though the startup has focused on monetisation and profitability, it has made sure that these revenue sources do not dilute the trust the brand has built amongst its viewers.

During the initial days, it was tough for the team to get money to organise large-scale events, but they didn't give up. They looked for creative ways to fund their events. When Josh Talks was organising India's largest youth conference—LEAP—in 2016, their budget had reached ₹35 lakh. It was a two-day event in which many known innovators, designers, artists, entrepreneurs, business leaders, thinkers, dreamers and changemakers were participating as speakers to share their remarkable ideas and stories. The team had worked for six months for the event's preparation. Unfortunately, even with only three days left for the event, no sponsors had been confirmed. The team was about to cancel the event. They thought that, with this, not only would the brand fail but so would their dream.

The team thought of trying out one final idea, as if following Milton Berle's precious advice of 'If opportunity doesn't knock, build a door'. Instead of getting seven sponsors, who could pay ₹5 lakh each, the team decided to create 70 stalls for ₹50,000 each. Within three days, 70 stalls lined up. These included a number of food stalls serving multiple cuisines as well as stalls showcasing entrepreneurship. With this, the team was able to fund their event. The team also created special discount packages for corporate employees and reached out to HR managers at various organisations. At last, 24 speakers graced the event, and over 5,000 audience members participated. The event turned out to be a massive success for the team.

Josh Talks provides its online content free to millions of people. The videos are viewed because of their compelling content. The wider the audience becomes, the higher the brand awareness and advocacy around the subject. To support the business, the company monetises through both online and offline revenue channels. The online revenue comes from brand partnerships and YouTube advertisements, and the offline revenue comes from event tickets and co-created properties with sponsors.

Initially, building revenue channels was not a cakewalk. To get partners, Supriya and the team would make over a hundred calls daily to HR and marketing contacts at companies. They did this for nearly two years and eventually, their persistence paid off. Their big break came in 2017 when Facebook came on board as the first partner and provided financial support. Over time, Josh Talks has been able to develop partnerships with many organisations, including Facebook India, ITC Vivel, United Nations, Oxfam, the Government of Arunachal Pradesh, the Office of the Chief Electoral Officer of Meghalaya, Reliance Industries, United Colours of Benetton, Amity University and a few others.

When people start loving and respecting a brand, it becomes the brand's responsibility to maintain the trust of its users. For life decisions, people trust very few sources, such as parents, siblings, teachers and mentors. To get into a similar space and to keep the trust in the brand intact, the company believes in protecting the brand's authenticity. It follows a fundamental rule that no sponsors are allowed to display logos in YouTube videos. In a few non-YouTube properties where logos are shown, neither sponsors nor speakers are allowed to sell anything during the talk or at a sponsored event.

Furthermore, the company associates itself with particular brands whose ethos or programmes are cause-related. For example, to raise awareness and enable conversation on women's rights, ITC Vivel collaborated with Josh Talks for its CSR initiative *Ab Samjhauta Nahin*. Under this property, workshops were organised in over 700 colleges around topics like workplace harassment, rape and cybersecurity.

Also, along with Facebook, Josh Talks has started a movement called #Startअब to inculcate an entrepreneurial spirit in the youth of India. #Startअब city events are an extension of Josh Talks conferences and take place across tier-2 and tier-3 cities in India with eight to ten speakers per conference and 500 live attendees. #Startअब workshops are designed specifically for colleges and serve as a hands-on introduction to the world of entrepreneurship and digital marketing. By May 2019, the team had completed over 300 #Startअब workshops in over 600 colleges, skilling more than 40,000 students with 1,000 plus hours of training.

Another example includes Josh Talks' partnership with UN Women's HearMeToo campaign that delved into violence against women in India and the effects it has on our society and the economy. Under this partnership, talks and panel discussions were organised with people who either had worked extensively in the space or had faced sexual harassment and violence in their lives and had overcome all their hardships to become inspirations for the world.

Strive to reach out to people

You must be wondering how two people in their twenties who had no relevant background managed to create one of the fastest-growing impact platforms in India. Success in any field is dependent on networks and relationships with the right set of people. To build this network, the Josh Talks team strives to reach out to people and builds strong relationships driven by the purpose of helping society at large.

While in college, Supriya and Shobhit would reach out to their teachers to help them get speakers and friends to contribute voluntarily for college events. Later on, the team met many café owners to find out about local achievers and invited them to speak at the events. When Nearbuy founder Ankur Warikoo attended one of the events as a speaker, he liked the event and enthusiasm of the team. Eventually, he became an adviser to Josh Talks and a mentor to the team. During the initial days, he also gave them space at his office for free.

When Josh Talks was organising the LEAP conference, the team attended numerous conferences and approached the speakers there to either speak at LEAP or connect them with other relevant speakers. Interestingly, one of the speakers connected them to the Bollywood director Anurag Kashyap. To invite one of the most influential comedians around the world, Papa CJ, Supriya and Shobhit attended six of his events and tried talking to him in the middle of the enormous crowd. Eventually, Papa CJ noticed them, spoke to them, and came to speak at the conference.

When Dr Ritesh Malik, founder of Innov8 Coworking (acquired by OYO), met Supriya and Shobhit, he was impressed by their passion. He came forward as an investor and guided the team on branding and networking. Similarly, Apurva Chamaria, chief revenue officer at RateGain, and Rana Atheya, founder of DogSpot, guided them on various aspects of the business.

To build credibility with the government, the team started networking with IAS officers and partnered with the Indian Army to get serving officers to speak on its platform. To get speakers and stories in bulk, the company has partnered with alumni cells and entrepreneurship cells at various engineering and MBA colleges, publishing houses, entrepreneurial groups, UPSC and CA coaching institutes, NGOs, social enterprises, news portals and many other organisations. As their speakers are the brand ambassadors of Josh Talks, they also connect the team with many different changemakers and potential speakers. For content distribution, the brand has partnered with various content platforms such as OLA Play, Dainik Bhaskar, iTunes, Saavn and JIO among others.

As Majhrooh Sultanpuri has written in his shayari, '*Main akela hi chala tha janib-e-manzil magar/log saath aate gaye aur karwaan banta gaya*', over time, the team has reached out to many people who have guided and helped them in various ways.

Help your team grow with you

In today's hypercompetitive world, relying on just founders for an organisation's growth is often inadequate. In fact, sometimes, many innovative ideas and fresh perspectives come from new team members and lead to remarkable initiatives and new markets.

In 2015, Supriya and Shobhit worked with interns and volunteers. By 2016, they had decided to move online, and since both of them have a non-technical background, getting the right team in place to build the product was a challenge. As Josh Talks was not a known brand then, it didn't have the luxury of choosing, but Supriya and Shobhit were hell-bent on the kind of people they wanted. Since the early days, they decided not to judge people based on their skills and the academic institutions they attended but on their passion.

As of May 2019, Josh Talks had a team of over 85 people with an average age of 23 years. Since the needs and the pains of the target audience are best understood by the target audience itself, many people are hired from amongst them. For example, the person responsible for app development comes from a village and is a self-taught coder. The organisation has different functions such as research, curation, events, production, distribution, operations, workshops, business strategy, Josh Kosh and others. There are people who lead each of these functions. By creating different functions and leaders, Supriya and Shobhit are able to delegate execution responsibilities and take out time to think about business growth.

The organisation has also created a special project team that is responsible for building new properties, conceptualising new ideas and taking them to a logical conclusion. To facilitate the flow of innovative ideas, Josh Talks has created an experiment group where team members share new ideas. To attract new ideas, every idea by the team members is listened to irrespective of its quality or practicality. Many organisations are not able to innovate because if something fails, people play the blame game. To avoid the blame game, Josh Talks has made it mandatory that a certain number of ideas in the experiment group have to fail every quarter.

To ensure existing platforms run efficiently, leaders have defined areas where their team members do not need their approvals. To scale their expertise and competence, the team has created checklists for every step involved in organising an event or a talk. Things such as how to look for and approach venues, sponsors, speakers, partners, etc. have been well documented. To identify and segment stories, different categories such as rags-to-riches stories, social causes, academia, sports, civil services, burning issues, trending topics, etc. have been created. Moreover, to bring out the unique aspects of stories, various sub-categories are created within every category. This documentation helps new team members deliver more talks in more venues with the expected quality.

As Josh Talks speakers come from all walks of life, the team has developed a standard process to coach their speakers to deliver a compelling and engaging story in 12–15 minutes.

One of the significant challenges for the company has been understanding the various regions, as each of them is different not only in terms of the language spoken but also the interests and aspirations of the audiences. To scale in regional languages, Josh Talks has hired team members from different areas who have an understanding of their regions and can converse with potential speakers and help them curate their speeches. Many of these team members come from underprivileged backgrounds but have been able to grow with the company. For instance, one of the regional language curators used to be a carpenter. Because of his passion and command over the Hindi language, he was hired and groomed to work as a curator.

To identify great stories, the team members create various combinations of relevant keywords and look even till the last pages of Google's search results. They keep an eye on every regional news source and even the non-popular YouTube videos of changemakers. The team reads every comment on their social media platforms and, based on the demand, creates new categories and initiatives. To ensure every video reaches as many viewers as possible, the team focuses on the consistency, timing and packaging of the videos. Besides, they continuously experiment with thumbnails, headlines, keywords and timing and extensively analyse the resulting data.

With the combined efforts of its team members, over the years, Josh Talks has become one of the most popular talk platforms in India and is continuously expanding to new vernacular languages. Moreover, the team has created many career-related and skill-building initiatives, such as a mentoring app through which achievers in various fields answer the questions of aspirants in their respective areas within 48 hours. Furthermore, an initiative like Josh Dialogue has been created to interview many known personalities, and a Professional Speaker Bureau has been started to bring event speakers from all areas of expertise together.

Apna Time Aayega, the song from the Bollywood movie *Gully Boy*, has become a motivational anthem for all those who dream of making it big in their lives.

The powerful lyrics of the song have the power to encourage people and give them hope. By creating an ecosystem to help the youth go from where they are to where they want to be, Josh Talks is nurturing, amplifying and materialising the belief of Apna Time Aayega. It would be interesting to see how this brand evolves and makes its mark in India's future.

SUPRIYA PAUL

Advice from Supriya Paul

- Identify your target audience, understand them well, and come up with a strategy to engage them with a long-term and sustainable marketing approach.
- Hire people who believe in your vision, don't just hire based on degrees. During tough times, people with elite degrees will leave, but people with a belief in your vision will stay and can help you in your come back.
- Don't be in a hurry to raise funds. First, identify your market and test your product and then get investors on board.
- Think about building relationships. Most of the time, people think about what they could get from others; instead, find ways to help others. When you help others, they often help you.
- Ask specific questions. The more specific you get, the easier it becomes for people to answer them and help you.
- To have the right co-founder with a similar vision is extremely important. When you feel like giving up, your co-founder can help you with their motivation and complementary skillset.

epigamia

Encouraging a healthy lifestyle without compromising on taste

Names like Satya Nadella, Sundar Pichai, Indra Nooyi and Ajay Banga have inspired many Indians. They have made India proud and their journeys deserve to be celebrated. However, there is also a need to share the journeys of Indians who were doing great in developed countries like the USA but returned to India and made their mark.

One such journey is that of Rohan Mirchandani who grew up in America, earned his education from prestigious institutions such as NYU's Stern School of Business, and The Wharton School of the University of Pennsylvania, and left a lucrative career in finance to come to India and become a food entrepreneur. In 2015, he launched India's first Greek yoghurt brand—Epigamia.

As per media reports, Epigamia has received significant funding from investors like Belgium-based consumer investment firm Verlinvest, Singapore-based fund DSG Consumer Partners, Temasek-backed InnoVen Capital, and French food giant Danone's investment arm Danone Manifesto Ventures. Furthermore, a few business leaders, including Cipla's Executive Vice Chairperson Samina Hamied and Bollywood actress Deepika Padukone, have also invested in Epigamia.

In its brief journey, Epigamia has received multiple awards, including Global Logistics Excellence Award for supply chain excellence in dairy products (organised by Infinity Expo with CNBC TV18) and Cold Chain Industry Award for the best distribution network strategy (organised by Future Supply Chain). Moreover, in 2018, Rohan received the Entrepreneur of the Year (Consumer Business) award from Entrepreneur India.

This chapter encapsulates the journey of Epigamia, India's fastest-growing Greek yoghurt brand.

THE BEGINNING

By 2008, Rohan had quit a budding career in finance and had taken the GMAT with an aspiration to get into an ivy league business school. During this period, he visited India and, along with his childhood friend Milap Shah, was contemplating starting a food venture. By chance, the duo happened to meet Chef Ganesh Krishnamoorthy, who had over two decades of experience in the food and beverage industry with a specialisation in Italian cuisine, including Italian ice cream, better known as gelato.

The trio joined hands to start Drums Food International and launched a premium ice cream brand Hokey Pokey. As a differentiator in the crowded ice cream market, Hokey Pokey had a live kitchen in its parlours, where customers could get their own ice cream flavours, created on a cold stone using different delicious ingredients. Now, a few other companies have entered this space, but Hokey Pokey was a pioneer.

When Rohan was selected for the MBA programme at Wharton, both Chef Ganesh and Milap were also involved in other businesses. With everyone busy, they hired a local management team to continue running Hokey Pokey, and Rohan returned to the USA for his MBA.

While pursuing his MBA, Rohan spent a week in Mumbai for a course on marketing to the Indian consumer. One of the guest lecturers was Shripad Nadkarni, a former marketing head at Coca-Cola, India. Rohan spoke with Shripad about his plan to spread Hokey Pokey's ice cream parlours across the country, but Shripad suggested to Rohan that he should focus on creating an FMCG brand instead of creating a retail chain.

There were multiple reasons behind the preference for an FMCG model over the retail model. Firstly, ice cream is a seasonal product, with demand peaking during the summer months. In this situation, the stores would not have significant sales during the winter and rainy seasons, but the rent would still have to be paid monthly and would increase annually. Secondly, to manage customer experience, retail stores need well-trained front-end staff. During the non-seasonal period, if good employees were underutilised, they could leave. Repeatedly hiring and training new employees would not be a feasible option. Thirdly, setting up individual stores in different areas would be a slow process. So, Rohan was able to follow a more practical approach through the FMCG model.

Shripad agreed to mentor Rohan and invest in the business on the condition that Rohan move to India and run the business full-time. After completing his MBA, Rohan had two options. He could either take up a well-paid corporate job in the USA or move to India. This was not an easy decision to make, due to the challenges faced by people in India like the lack of infrastructure, amongst other. However, Rohan decided to follow Shripad's advice. In January 2013, at the age of 30, Rohan moved to India to focus on making Hokey Pokey a success.

He, along with the team, started building the FMCG plan for Hokey Pokey. They hit the stores in 2014 and, within a short period, Hokey Pokey became a famous ice cream brand known for its unique flavours. But as ice cream is a seasonal product, sales plummeted during the monsoon and winter months, and distribution expansion during the off-season became a massive challenge.

To ensure sustained growth of the business and to avoid dependency on a particular season, the team decided to start a non-seasonal product along with their ice creams. In 2015, Drums Food International launched the Greek yoghurt brand Epigamia, which was something unique for the Indian markets. While it was launched as a complementary product to ice cream, since it was healthier and still delicious, the Greek yoghurt proved to be a sleeper hit. The brand saw sales of 10,000 cups within the first month of launch.

Though the team wanted to grow both the ice cream and the Greek yoghurt businesses, there were multiple operational challenges in running both of them parallelly. For instance, ice cream requires a frozen supply chain, while yoghurt needs a cold supply chain. With limited resources, managing two different supply chains was not a viable option. Also, Greek yoghurt has a shelf life of only 15 days, unlike ice creams which have a shelf life of 9–12 months. This meant that both products had different requirements for production, storage and distribution.

Though Hokey Pokey had become a leading premium ice cream brand, managing its day-to-day operations along with creating growth opportunities for Epigamia was not practically possible. With Indian consumers aiming for a healthier lifestyle, Greek yoghurt appeared to be a significant and untapped opportunity as compared to ice cream. So, working along John D. Rockerfeller's quote—'Don't be afraid to give up the good to go for the great'—the team decided to focus only on Epigamia and discontinued Hokey Pokey temporarily.

THE BRAND NAME: EPIGAMIA

It is essential to come up with a brand name that has a good recall value. If a famous story with a universal appeal lies at the root of a brand's name, it can amplify it. This is what worked well for Epigamia.

In 326 BCE, Alexander the Great, a ruler of the ancient Greek kingdom of Macedonia, after conquering much of Persia, launched his campaign to enter India. After Alexander's death in 323 BCE, Chandragupta Maurya, with the guidance of Chanakya, established a strong empire in India, which came to be known as the Mauryan dynasty.

In 312 BCE, Seleucus I Nicator, a Macedonian general from Alexander's army, established the Seleucid Kingdom and reconquered most of Alexander's former empire in Asia. In 305 BCE, he came into conflict with Chandragupta. Eventually, both sides made peace in 303 BCE. In ancient Greek, Epigamia was a way of formalising the relationship between different nations. This peace treaty was known as Epigamia, standing for a dynastic marriage between the two wonderful and ancient cultures. As a result, a flourishing exchange of ideas and trade began between the two empires.

To celebrate this ancient tradition, by being the first to introduce Greek yoghurt in India, the team decided to name the brand Epigamia. Epigamia, the brand that weds a healthy lifestyle to great taste.

BUSINESS LESSONS

Many valuable lessons can be learnt from the evolution of Epigamia. Here are some of the important things that we can learn from this brand's journey.

Don't let the opinions of others distract you

Steve Jobs said, 'Your time is limited, so don't waste it living someone else's life. Don't be trapped by dogma—which is living with the results of other people's thinking. Don't let the noise of others' opinions drown out your own inner voice. And most important, have the courage to follow your heart and intuition.' Rohan's journey is a testament to this quote.

Typically, everyone in your family and social circle expects you to take up a fancy corporate job if you went to a top business school. Rohan was expected to do the same, after he graduated from Wharton. But, disappointing many people around him, he chose entrepreneurship and that too in India. Many of his friends warned him that he was taking a huge risk, and getting back to a corporate career would be difficult. However, Rohan felt that taking up a corporate job for status and prestige would put him in a comfort zone, from which it would be difficult for him emerge later.

Many of his relatives considered his decision insane and said, '*Tumhara dimaag kharaab ho gaya hai*.' They tried educating him about all the possible problems he could face in an unorganised market like India. But instead of listening to what other's had to say, Rohan decided to listen to his heart, which told him that he should focus on creating a globally respected Indian brand.

When they realised that Rohan was determined to become an entrepreneur, many people suggested that he start an IT firm. Despite knowing that IT companies can quickly become high-valuation businesses, Rohan knew that technology was not his forte. He didn't want to start a venture in the IT sector just because others were making money in it. Instead, due to his passion for food, he wanted to enter the FMCG industry. Apart from his personal interest, Rohan realised that the Indian food and beverage market was at a nascent stage then and with the way India was growing, he sensed there would be massive opportunities in the sector.

Even before he went for his MBA, Rohan had already started an ice cream brand in Indian called Hokey Pokey, which he decided to grow through the FMCG route. When he decided to return to India, he prepared himself to expect challenges. He came with a vision and an agenda but with zero expectations. He was clear that he would be persistent, and even if he failed in this venture, he would gain invaluable learnings.

Interestingly, in its first year of operation, the ice cream business grew 100 per cent, and Hokey Pokey became a much-loved brand. However, before Rohan could scale-up the business, new challenges emerged. Ice cream sales would drop during the non-seasonal period, and while the team tried managing the situation for a few years, the business began running out of money. Eventually, the company decided to discontinue the ice cream business. Many people considered it a failure, but for Rohan it was a learning experience.

When Rohan decided to focus on the Greek yoghurt business singlemindedly, many people could not understand his decision. '*Wharton ka ladka dahi bech raha hain*,' they would say. Moreover, many retailers were not interested in giving him shelf space. '*Yeh nahi chalega*,' they told him. But after a lot of follow-ups and conversations, Rohan and his team managed to convince shopkeepers to give their product shelf space.

Within a short span of four years, Epigamia was selling over 3 million cups of Greek yoghurt monthly through e-commerce websites like BigBasket and Amazon, retail chains like Godrej Natures Basket, Future Group, Reliance Retail and D-Mart, through numerous kirana stores and even hotel chains such as the Taj Group, Crown Plaza, Marriott and Westin. With his persistence and passion, Rohan had created the foundation of the Greek yoghurt category in India and, in the process, had established Epigamia as a fresh FMCG brand with the attributes of good taste, quality and health.

Create a space in consumers' lives

In today's fast-paced world, consumers have countless choices, and their brand preferences change quickly. Rohan says, 'To stay relevant in such a competitive scenario, identifying your target audience, understanding them deeper, and creating a space in their lives are absolute necessities.'

In India, dahi (curd) has a unique space in people's lives. Most of us have grown up with dahi as a part of our daily diet, where it is served with hot parathas for breakfast and with khichdi or as curd rice for lunch or dinner. Also, a bowl of curd is always served with a thali meal. It is a nutritious and light food item with numerous health benefits. When dahi is prepared at Indian homes, we see a layer of water over it, which is known as whey. Greek yoghurt is a thicker and smoother version of the Indian dahi. It is prepared by draining excess whey, which helps give it a thicker consistency. This process further involves mechanised mixing so that the product becomes smooth and creamy. Greek yoghurt is a tasty yet healthy product that contains the nutrients that we typically fall short on, such as protein and calcium. To get an equivalent amount of protein from regular dahi, one would need to consume double the quantity.

Interestingly, Rohan was exposed to Greek yoghurt for the first time in the USA. One evening, he had ordered a sandwich and chips at a deli in New York City. The deli manager suggested that he try Greek yoghurt instead of chips. Rohan liked it very much and felt that the Greek yoghurt filled his stomach. This made him research Greek yoghurt, and he found that it was a natural, healthy and protein-rich lifestyle product that could be consumed daily.

Looking at the potential of the product, the target market of older millennials intrigued Rohan. He felt that customers in this segment, including new-age couples living in urban cities, were more health-conscious than their younger counterparts. He found that though the trend to eat fresh and healthy was on the rise, the options available were limited. Also, while snacks like samosas and chips were readily available, healthy snacks were not. When it came to desserts too, ice creams, cakes and mithais contained artificial flavours and preservatives, and while a few healthier options were available, they lacked taste.

Through a deeper understanding of the market, Rohan realised that a snacking option that is both healthy and delicious had immense potential. People eat snacks for breakfast and during evenings, usually between 4 p.m. to 6 p.m. when small hunger strikes. Considering the importance of dahi in people's lives, Rohan felt that Greek yoghurt (a contemporary, modern-day twist on the popular dahi) could serve as a snack, a tasty accompaniment or even a dessert. It meets much of our daily protein need and can promote weight loss, as it can make people feel full for extended periods between meals. Rohan decided to position his yoghurts as a solution for the 'Choti si bhook' problem and launched India's first Greek yoghurt brand—Epigamia. The uniqueness of Epigamia's Greek yoghurt is that it contains no preservatives and artificial flavours and has a natural taste. A pack of 90 gm yoghurt holds 160 calories and claims to provide the protein intake equivalent of 1.5 eggs or two cups of dal, apart from being 99 per cent lactose-free. To stimulate the taste buds, real fruit is mixed in the yoghurt. Over time, Epigamia launched multiple variants of the Greek yoghurt with flavours like mango, vanilla, honey banana, blueberry, green apple, strawberry and mulberry.

In 2017, Epigamia launched Snack Pack with unique flavours and the nutritional benefits of protein and fibre. It introduced unconventional combinations, such as Jalapeño Greek Yoghurt with Fibre-Rich Barley Puffs, Mango Greek Yoghurt with Chunky Granola and Strawberry Greek Yoghurt with Chunky Granola. The brand has also launched many other products such as preservative-free smoothies, which are just like lassi but with the added fuel of high protein and real fruits for stimulating taste. In due course of time, Epigamia has been able to create a place in its consumers' lives as a hero of small hunger.

Disrupt a market, even if initially small

To create a successful business, an entrepreneur's first challenge is to create a great product, and the second challenge is to get it accepted by the appropriate market. While products like Greek yoghurt and smoothies fall under the category of dairy products, Rohan decided to position Epigamia as a healthy snack brand and not necessarily as a health food or dairy brand.

Snacks have been a part of our daily lives, and most popular snack items have been junk foods like chips, burgers, samosas, chocolates and namkeens. However, powered by higher disposable income and increasing health consciousness, India's growing urban middle-class population is becoming interested in pursuing mental wellness, physical fitness and a balanced diet. Rohan decided to target this segment for Epigamia.

To begin with, Rohan focused on promoting the sampling of the product. Trying samples is a risk-free way for shoppers to try new products without committing to buy. He visited hundreds of modern trade and kirana stores in Mumbai to get space for the products and to put up sampling counters. Initially, there was a lot of push back from retailers in terms of giving space to a new brand. But Rohan persisted and asked shopkeepers to taste his product. Eventually, around 200 stores in prime locations agreed to give space to Epigamia.

Along with his team, Rohan invested a lot of time in capturing the reviews of shoppers and analysing daily and weekly sales. His team was swift in terms of replacing the unsold stock and slow-moving variants with fast-selling variants. Rohan took the feedback of shopkeepers and shoppers seriously and made every attempt to delight them through his product and service. For instance, once when a retailer called Rohan to tell him that a customer had liked one of the products and was asking for more, but the product was not available with the retailer, Rohan went out of his way to deliver the desired variants to the customer that very same night.

After analysing the response from the stores in Mumbai for nine months, Rohan scaled up the sampling activity to Bengaluru and Chennai, followed by Delhi and then Hyderabad. To speed things up in the new cities, Rohan started reaching out to city-based retailer associations to get access to multiple kirana stores. Many retailers told him that they had not seen a newspaper advertisement or billboard for Epigamia, and that they would not keep an unknown brand in their stores. Rohan didn't have money for advertisements then, but to gain the mindshare of reluctant retailers, the team got the brand's advertisement placed in a local newspaper and got billboards placed in areas from where those retailers used to travel. Through this two-month trial campaign targeted at retailers, Epigamia was able to scale-up its presence from 200 to 1,200 stores.

To appeal to the health-conscious audience and get reviews and endorsements, the team planned to get the products sampled at pro-health events and places such as marathons, yoga centres and gyms. The team also targeted health and fitness events. For instance, Epigamia co-hosted an event for the Indian Dietetic Association's Mumbai chapter to celebrate World Health Day. Furthermore, to make Epigamia part of the breakfast menu at popular high-end restaurants, Chef Ganesh shared the product with chefs in those restaurants, who eventually shared their positive views with purchase managers. To capture the target audience at airports and hotels, Epigamia did six months of sample promotions at metro airports and at premium and luxury hotels.

Food bloggers and nutritionists play a significant role in influencing food habits, and no food and beverage company should avoid their platforms. To collaborate with them, the team ran multiple campaigns in which food bloggers and nutritionists talked about the benefits of Greek yoghurt and many exciting ways in which yoghurt can be used in day-to-day meals. Pictures of exciting dishes created with Epigamia yoghurt started going viral on Instagram, and the brand's popularity saw an upswing.

As Epigamia's core target audience is millennials, who consume a lot of content on the internet in comparison to the TV, the team took the digital content creation route to reach them. Epigamia partnered with Pocket Aces, a digital entertainment company, for the web series *What the Folks*. In August 2017, Season 1 was released with Epigamia as the title partner and was a massive hit with over 30 million views. This web series gave Epigamia high ROI in terms of brand awareness amongst consumers. Later on, Season 2 became a perfect platform for Epigamia to launch new products such as Greek Yoghurt Smoothies, lactose-free curd and Mishti Doi.

In 2019, not only did Bollywood actress Deepika Padukone became the brand ambassador for Epigamia, she also invested in the company. As Epigamia is now in the process of expanding across India, it is investing in ATL campaigns spread across TV, print, outdoor and online formats with Deepika as the new face of the brand.

Focus on building relationships, not just on transactions

Many people relate to other people when making a transaction or a business deal. Once the deal is done, they may not connect with the other person until they are ready for another transaction. But businesses are built mainly on relationships, not transactions. Because he is relationship-oriented, Rohan has been able to find many supporters and has been able to create a strong team.

While founding Hokey Pokey, Rohan was able to convince Chef Ganesh to join part-time, as he had a well-paying job. Later on, when Rohan came back to India after doing his MBA, he pursued Chef Ganesh for almost eight months to join the business full-time. Seeing Rohan's passion and his focus on making Hokey Pokey a success, Chef Ganesh left his job and joined Epigamia full-time. With the support of Chef Ganesh, Rohan was able to make Hokey Pokey one of the leading brands in India's premium ice cream market. The brand also introduced the innovative concept of interactive ice cream counters.

A few people who had seen Rohan's passion and commitment while running Hokey Pokey came forward to support him in Epigamia's journey. One of the early supporters was Manu Chandra, founder of early-stage VC fund Sauce.vc. He had taken up two franchisees of Hokey Pokey stores, which were eventually shut down as Rohan decided to discontinue that brand. Even though Manu had lost his investment in Hokey Pokey, he invested in Epigamia. Manu says he funded the business because he liked Rohan's limitless passion and determination, focus on product and brand, and his ability to attract people to support him. He has been impressed by Rohan's attitude and courage to fail fast, learn and recover. Even though the business has grown and many new investors have come on board, Rohan makes sure that he meets his early investors and sounding boards—Shripad and Manu—once a month for dinner.

Another person with whom Rohan had developed a relationship while running Hokey Pokey was Rahul Jain, who was the founder of an organic milk brand, Doctor Moo. Rahul had approached Rohan in order to sell him milk for ice creams. Though the deal did not materialise, they became friends. When Rahul was looking to launch new product lines, he discussed Greek yoghurt with Rohan. Since Rohan was looking to expand his team, they joined hands, and Rahul joined Epigamia as a co-founder.

Similarly, Rohan had been in touch with Ramanpreet Sohi, who worked with a private equity fund where Rohan had pitched to raise funds for Hokey Pokey. Despite the fact that the deal did not go through, Rohan and Ramanpreet remained in touch. When Rohan was looking for someone to head finance, he checked with Ramanpreet, who joined Epigamia as its CFO. To build the distribution network, Rohan needed someone with substantial experience in marketing and distribution. Through Shripad, he met Siddarth Menon, who had worked in leadership roles with global FMCG brands and was looking to do something different. For some time, Siddarth was partially involved and then eventually joined Epigamia as its CMO.

As we have already discussed, Rohan invested time in building relationships with retailers in Mumbai by meeting them in person, serving 24X7, providing products on time, taking back expired products, and acting on customer complaints immediately. Over time, Epigamia has built a team that regularly meets retailers and checks the status of the stock. Furthermore, the Epigamia team has focused on building relationships with various stakeholders in the ecosystem like supply chain partners and vendors.

Biz Stone has said, 'Positive culture comes from being mindful, and respecting your co-workers, and being empathetic.' On similar lines, Rohan has been focused on creating an ambitious and empathetic culture within the organisation. Epigamia runs a unique two-year programme in which youngsters join the company to work with the CEO office directly. In this period, they work as the CEO's ears and eyes on the ground and get exposure to various aspects of running an FMCG business. With this rich exposure, many of the programme participants get into business schools, get jobs in FMCG companies or grow within Epigamia. Some of the alumni of this programme have gone on to work for VC funds like Verlinvest and Sequoia, while others are attending business schools such as INSEAD and London Business School.

To keep a check on the organisational culture, the company has created an innovative new role—manager of culture and ecosystem. The job of this manager is to create and manage a feedback loop within the organisation, keep an eye on people's engagement, communicate with employees and keep Rohan updated about people's motivation levels. With the help of the manager of culture and ecosystem, Rohan makes sure that nobody is bored and the office is a fun place to work.

Before scaling up, stabilise your business

Marcel Telles said, 'A company can seize extraordinary opportunities only if it is very good at the ordinary operations.' Rohan and his team invested foundational years in stabilising the back-end operations, which have evolved with time.

Initially, the team tried distributing Greek yoghurt through third-party distributors. However, it soon realised that the cold chain network in India was broken. For Greek yoghurt, which has a shelf life of 15 days, the clock starts ticking as soon as the product is ready. When Epigamia was a small brand and distributors were focused on catering to established brands, they did not prioritise Epigamia's deliveries to retailers, and the product often expired before it was sold.

The team decided to create its own distribution network. Rahul Jain, one of the co-founders and the COO of Epigamia, had created an innovative cold chain-based home-delivery business model while studying at ISB. He had started delivering fresh organic milk to homes in Mumbai in 2013 and had scaled it up to 5,000 homes by 2015. Epigamia replicated that model. As of June 2019, the company had 100 cold-chain trucks, with each covering 25–30 stores every day. Sales staff accompany each truck to ensure that the products are placed in the correct refrigerated shelves. As the company is targeting new cities, it is investing in scaling up its cold chain infrastructure.

Setting up a back-end supply chain was not easy. Rohan would sit for hours in the offices of large milk dairies but didn't get the necessary support. Eventually, he found a few startup milk dairies that had the required infrastructure. Epigamia invested in technology, processes, equipment, etc. and got these dairies to function as its dedicated production facilities. Also, to set up a supply chain for real fruits from farms, Chef Ganesh's contacts, of farmers in various regions of India, came in handy.

Innovation is at the core of Epigamia's business. The company has an innovation centre, which is like an R&D lab. Though Epigamia is not a technology company, it follows a technology-driven approach. All new products go through alpha and beta testing. The consumer insights team collects feedback from current customers, potential customers, global and domestic trends, and continuously updates Chef Ganesh for the products pipeline. Chef Ganesh filters the product opportunities based on Epigamia's promise of no preservatives and all-natural ingredients.

At the lab scale, Chef Ganesh does bench trials and, during the alpha phase, tests new products with internal stakeholders such as management and the marketing and sales teams. Based on internal stakeholders' feedback, if the product passes the alpha phase, it goes for beta testing. In the beta phase, the product is manufactured on a small scale and stocked at a selectively identified 200 to 250 stores in Mumbai, ranging from high-end supermarkets to kirana stores. These stores represent a sample of the broader market. The team captures data on the sales of new products. During this phase, the product is also shared with a selected group of food influencers. If they pass the product and if there is repeat purchase at stores, then the new product passes beta testing and goes through to the full phase production. Through its continuous innovation process, Epigamia has developed many unique and popular flavours such as wild raspberry, honey banana, pink guava and green apple.

Reid Hoffman said, 'The entrepreneurial journey starts with jumping off a cliff and assembling an airplane on the way down.' When Rohan started his entrepreneurial journey, he didn't have much context of the Indian market, but he jumped in with his faith and confidence.

When he started Hokey Pokey, Rohan didn't have any experience of running an ice cream business. Moreover, the market was already very crowded. Yet, he managed to create a well-known brand. Rohan had to shut down the ice cream retail business. This was followed by the closure of the FMCG business. However, Rohan didn't give up. When an opportunity appeared with Greek yoghurt, neither the market was aware of the product nor did Rohan and his team have prior experience creating the product. But with preparation, hard work and learning from failures, Rohan and his team managed to create India's largest-selling Greek yoghurt brand—Epigamia.

The company plans to expand within India and is looking to tap broader South Asia markets like Bangladesh, Sri Lanka and, eventually, the Middle East and Southeast Asia. With his ability to evolve by learning from his mistakes, Rohan has been able to assemble his airplane in the form of Epigamia. It would be interesting to watch this airplane flying through the global skies in the future!

ROHAN MIRCHANDANI

Advice from Rohan Mirchandani

- Your customer is beyond you and your friends. Just because you or your friends like something doesn't mean that it will work in the market. Validate your assumptions with feedback from real customers.
- Passion has to be the driving force behind your venture. Don't do something just because others are doing it or because the industry is glamorous.
- Advertising can bring in customers once, but for repeat purchases, you need to have a killer product.
- Instead of being afraid to fail, view failure as a learning experience. Though the ice cream business was closed down due to fundamentals, the experience of running Hokey Pokey gave a lot of insights on retail, FMCG and consumer experience. These insights became helpful in creating Epigamia.

ShareChat

Empowering non-English internet users

Thomas Friedman said, 'Big breakthroughs happen when what is suddenly possible meets what is desperately needed.' Utilising the power of the internet, social media networks like Facebook, LinkedIn, WhatsApp, Twitter and Instagram showed the world that it is possible to share ideas and create relationships with other people, no matter where they are—across the city or across the world. These leading social media networks were started in America and have English as the primary language of communication.

India has 22 official languages with 6,000 plus dialects. In such a diverse country, around 90 per cent of the population doesn't speak English, and it does not make sense to deprive this huge market from the internet revolution. Hence, a social network in various languages was desperately needed. To attract the next billion internet users from tier-2, tier-3 cities and rural India, global social media platforms have been tailoring their products. In parallel to the international players, this requirement made a few Indian startups create products specifically for the unserved non-English speaking users. One such product is ShareChat, a first-of-its-kind social media for consumers to be able to express themselves in their own mother tongue.

In 2015, three IIT Kanpur graduates, Ankush Sachdeva, Farid Ahsan and Bhanu Pratap Singh, came up with the concept of ShareChat. ShareChat has now become one of the fastest-growing startups in India, backed by investors like Twitter, Shunwei Capital, Morningside Ventures, Jesmond Holdings, Xiaomi, SAIF Partners, Lightspeed Venture Partners, Venture Highway and India Quotient.

During its brief journey, ShareChat and its founders have received numerous recognitions such as CNBC TV18 India Business Leader Awards (Young Turks Startup of the Year), TiE Lumis Entrepreneurial Excellence Award, Forbes 30 under 30 India, Forbes 30 under 30 Asia, India Content Leadership Award, Entrepreneur 35 under 35 and a few others. Also, the team has been part of the Google Launchpad Accelerator and INK Fellows Program.

This chapter encapsulates the journey of ShareChat, India's largest vernacular social network.

THE BEGINNING

Ankush, Farid and Bhanu were born into typical middle-class families and grew up in the tier-2 towns of Ghaziabad, Lucknow and Gorakhpur respectively. As often happens in middle-class families, their parents wanted them to become engineers and work in big multinational companies. And there is no place more famous than the Indian Institute of Technology (IITs) to help young people achieve these goals. Every year, lakhs of students appear for IITs' Joint Entrance Examination (JEE), but only a few thousand of them pass the test. Fortunately Ankush, Farid and Bhanu got into the prestigious IIT Kanpur.

As students at IIT Kanpur, they used to participate in hackathons, events where programmers meet for collaborative computer programming. At one of the hackathons—Yahoo Hack U—they met each other and discovered their love for building technology products. While at college, the trio worked on 13 product ideas. Unfortunately, these products didn't go anywhere.

Like the modern-day classic *3 Idiots*, which has become an inspiration for this generation, all three of them decided to be a part of the startup ecosystem rather than take up a job at a multinational company. They wanted to create a successful product for the Indian audience. Ankush says, 'I told my father that for a job, companies like Microsoft, Google, Amazon would exist even after five years, but I will not be the same person after five years because of my age and family responsibilities. If I don't pursue my passion now, then I would regret five years later.' Their parents were unhappy with their decision and expressed their inability to provide any financial support. Having faith in their dreams and themselves, they moved to Mumbai after graduation, to work on their 14th product—a chat platform.

In Mumbai, there was a different world waiting for them. They used to sleep in the office of a real-estate startup Grabhouse, founded by Prateek Shukla, their friend and senior from IIT Kanpur. During this period, the trio pitched their idea to many investors but didn't achieve any success. Prateek introduced them to Anand Lunia, the founding partner at an early-stage venture capital firm, India Quotient. Sadly, Anand also felt that their chat platform was not a product that Indians needed. He encouraged them to build something that would get new internet users hooked. In those penny-pinching days, Anand supported them by offering them a workspace in his office.

At the India Quotient office, its founding partner Madhukar Sinha became their unofficial mentor. He not only guided them but also shared his cabin and lunch with them. While working out of the India Quotient office, the trio created Opinio, a debating app where users could participate in time-bound debates on various topics. Though they wanted Indian users to debate on topics like Sachin Tendulkar vs Virat Kohli, a lot of users were from Europe, and the debates were around topics like nuclear disarmament and water scarcity. The product attracted 32,000 users in a few months but didn't grow any further. Unfortunately, Opinio became the trio's 15th failure.

In November 2014, the trio stumbled upon the idea of a vernacular content-sharing platform. This time, Anand and Madhukar saw potential in their product. In February 2015, fortune smiled at them. India Quotient became the first investor, funding the venture with $100,000. A further eight months of iterations led to the development of ShareChat in its current form.

THE BRAND NAME: SHARECHAT

There cannot be a more complicated process than choosing a name for a brand. A name that is very common leads to the brand getting lost in the crowd. What a brand needs is a unique name, but one that is easy to pronounce and that resonates with the target audience. Interestingly, meaningful and memorable names can be created by linking common words in a particular order.

As ShareChat's target audiences were non-English-speaking people, they wanted a name that could connect with people across India and, at the same time, was easy to search on Google Play Store. Initially, the team thought of the name ChaiTime because of the popularity of the words 'chai' and 'time' across India. This name sounded very casual and was not suitable for formal use cases such as finding jobs and any other serious business, as Indians don't take teatime gossip seriously.

Interestingly, while watching people conversing on WhatsApp groups, the team found that 'share' and 'chat' were two famous English words in the vocabulary of even non-English-speaking person. They linked these two words and created the brand name—ShareChat. This name resonates with the non-English-speaking crowd; it is easy to search on the Google Play Store; it has a positioning of an internet-based brand and it also has the seriousness to encompass new use cases in the future.

BUSINESS LESSONS

There are many important business lessons that can be learnt from the evolution of ShareChat. A few of them are as follows.

Develop an attitude to hustle and iterate

What separates hustlers from non-achievers is how they respond to failures. Hustlers learn from their failures, get back on their feet, and iterate execution to achieve their goals. Non-achievers, on the other hand, simply give up. The ShareChat team believes in being hustlers.

Before ShareChat, the team worked on 15 products but none of those worked out. For instance, in 2012, the team developed a real-estate portal similar to Housing.com, but it was not successful. The company was based in Kanpur and the low internet bandwidth there proved to be a disadvantage. Moreover, it was not possible for a Kanpur-based company to compete with well-funded real-estate portals in cities like Mumbai and Delhi. The venture was discontinued. Later, while still in college, the team tried building a data analytics company. As a use case, they developed a crime analysis system for the Delhi Police using all the FIRs posted online. This system had the capability to generate crime-specific location-based heat maps.

The trio travelled to Delhi to meet the Police Commissioner. Starting from the lowest grade officer in the morning, the trio pitched to the Assistant Commissioner of Police (ACP) by the evening. The ACP was impressed with the prototype and assured them that he would support their project. After getting this assurance, the trio came back to Kanpur to convert their prototype into a fully functional product. They formed a team of 21 students to work on this project. In this excitement, a few students started skipping classes. Noticing their absence, one of the professors complained to the Dean. The Dean's office called the parents of Ankush, Farid and Bhanu and informed them that their sons were not studying and were also distracting other students. Fortunately, the trio had not paid any money to the other students for participating in this project. As there was no financial transaction involved, Ankush, Farid and Bhanu were not terminated.

The incident led to the team of 21 students splitting up. However, Ankush, Bhanu and Farid stayed together. Unfortunately, there was a change in the government in Delhi, and the ACP who had been a ray of hope for them was transferred. The project no longer seemed to have a future so the trio moved on to another project. They created a game and launched it during the annual festival at IIT Kanpur. The team created a 15-page manual for the game, but they found that no one was interested in reading it. As people didn't read the manual, they were not able to progress beyond the first level and left the game in frustration. This experience taught the trio that a product meant for the mass market had to be simple enough to be understood without a manual.

As their next project, the team built a language-agnostic recipe-discovery product. Using this product, an Indian could learn to make French dishes without knowing French. But once again, no one really needed it.

Around Valentine's Day, the trio came up with an idea of a dating product—Puppy Love. Initially, no one showed interest in the project, and students were sceptical about the security of their personal information captured by the application. To address the concerns of the students, the team created a fully secure encryption layer in the application and ran a Q&A campaign on Quora. Eventually, the product was launched, and 40 per cent of the students on the campus used it on the first day of the launch. It became an instant hit and the talk of the campus, and around 50 couples met each other using this application. Though the feedback turned from negative to positive, and the product showed results, the team realised that the product had limited potential and decided to let it remain a fun college project. The trio created many other products that, unfortunately, didn't work out any better.

While working on their 15th failed product Opinio, the trio came across a Facebook post that asked people to share their phone numbers if they were keen on being added to a WhatsApp group about Sachin Tendulkar. There were over 50,000 responses. Looking at this, they put up similar posts on Facebook and quickly made a tool that could create WhatsApp groups and scrape thousands of phone numbers from Facebook posts, and left for lunch. When they returned, each group was buzzing with hundreds of messages. More revealingly, none of the messages were in English. The trio was drawn to the scope of business of vernacular content in India.

This experiment led to the creation of an app that would cater to the non-English-speaking population, thrive on user-generated content and have a social networking component. Today, the ShareChat app has become India's topmost regional language social media platform.

Thomas Edison said, 'Our greatest weakness lies in giving up. The most certain way to succeed is always to try just one more time.' Ankush, Farid and Bhanu worked on 15 failed products before ShareChat, but with every failure they learnt something new that gave them the ability to succeed.

Create a product or service that people want

Despite best efforts, the vast majority of products fail to achieve adoption by their target customers because these products are outcomes of the entrepreneurs' assumptions, not the customers' expectations. Figuring out what customers want is not as easy as it sounds. It is a tough process that requires a lot of observation and experimentation.

For long, internet-based products like social networking sites were created for the English-speaking world. But with the advent of affordable internet connectivity and broader network coverage, a large population that is not comfortable with English is slowly coming online. According to a March 2017 report by Google and KPMG, users comfortable in their own languages in India were expected to grow to 536 million by 2021, as against 199 million for English.

Thus the next billion online users were expected to come from tier-2, tier-3, tier-4 towns and villages. At the time of the study, many of these people wouldn't even have had email addresses and might have yet to experience the internet through smartphones. It is possible that WhatsApp, rather than Facebook, Twitter and Instagram, would be the first social network they access. Many of them wouldn't have heard about Yahoo or have searched on Google. A large number of these new internet users would come from the bottom of the pyramid (BOP) and would have different language preferences, different content requirements, and different user behaviour from the urban and English-speaking internet users.

Global social networks look at India as a huge business opportunity; and to capture users of vernacular languages they have been tailor-making their products. But all of India is not like the English-friendly urban India that embraced Western social networking sites. Different regions have different festivals, cultures, food preferences and dresses. There are more than 70,000 newspapers printed in India, and around 90 per cent are either printed in Hindi or different vernacular languages. There are numerous TV channels in languages like Bundeli, Maithili, Chhattisgarhi, Bhojpuri, Assamese, Konkani and others. Moreover, regional film industries and radio channels are experiencing significant growth. These examples clearly show that a lot of possibilities will emerge when these audiences with diverse expectations and behaviours come on to social media networks.

It is really important to understand that only a person who has witnessed the day-to-day life of rural India and towns can understand the dynamics and requirements of the people there. The folks living in metros can talk about it all they want, but they do not comprehend the complexities of the majority of India. All three—Ankush, Bhanu and Farid—come from small towns and have studied in Kanpur for four years, so they understand the thought process of people in small cities. Furthermore, once every quarter, they visit small towns to see what is happening on the ground. For instance, in 2017, Ankush took a trip to the hinterlands of the Rajasthan–Haryana border, where he observed a rapidly growing internet user base, with at least one smartphone in every home. Similarly, when the team took a trip to Kerala to study user behaviour, they found stark differences between the behaviours, aspirations and interests of users from North and South Kerala. With its on-ground research and interactions, the team found that a fresh stream of new internet users was pouring in, and their behaviours and expectations were very different from those of the existing ones.

To focus only on non-English-speaking audiences, ShareChat removed its English language option and has been concentrating solely on vernacular languages. To get the initial traction, the team growth hacked by joining several WhatsApp groups where ShareChat content could be shared. ShareChat's early adopters were the members of over 1,000 WhatsApp groups. They wanted to share trendy regional content to look cool in their respective groups. To make sharing of content to WhatsApp hassle free, the functionality of one-touch WhatsApp sharing was created within ShareChat. A fresh stream of regional content like news, daily horoscope, poetry, government job notifications, satire on Indian politics, henna designs, etc. started flowing on WhatsApp, and the popularity of ShareChat as a source of regional content started increasing.

Each share had a link that would take the user to the Google Play Store. This led to WhatsApp users becoming ShareChat users as well. By December 2015, the ShareChat app had 1,00,000 installs. Furthermore, based on the feedback from Google Play Store and after looking at the people sharing content, the team opened the platform for users to create their own content. This resulted in content being generated by regular users of the app, such as astrologers from states like Rajasthan, local language news outlets in states like Uttar Pradesh, and programmers building games in cities like Bengaluru and others. The platform made these interactions as smooth and as personalised as possible.

Over time, the team found that people express themselves differently in different languages. So, the team created new features for them. For example, each language may have its own unique expression or term that captures the essence of admiration, excitement or excellence, similar to the English word 'awesome'. On ShareChat, you can find different equivalents of the word 'awesome' in each Indian language. Another interesting example is ShareChat's selfie filters that have regional elements attached to them. New filters are launched depending on trending social events in different language markets. As of July 2019, ShareChat was available in 15 languages: Hindi, Punjabi, Bengali, Gujarati, Marathi, Telugu, Tamil, Malayalam, Bhojpuri, Odia, Kannada, Assamese, Rajasthani, Urdu and Haryanvi. With its ability to understand its users and unique features, ShareChat has managed to establish a lead in the vernacular social networking apps market with over 45 million monthly active users.

Empower your customers to bring more customers

Former Prime Minister of India Atal Bihari Vajpayee said, 'Empowering the individual means empowering the nation. And empowerment is best served through rapid economic growth with rapid social change.' And it can be seen that, ShareChat has been focusing on empowering its user base.

Initially, ShareChat became a regional language content source for users who started sharing the content on WhatsApp. When shared content started becoming popular, people wanted to put their names to the content they created. Looking at this need, an editing option that allowed users to attach their identity to their creations was added to the app. The team also found that people had a strong need to share images of themselves, so they created an option of adding a profile picture. To empower creators on the platform, the team created a followership model so that the audience could follow their favourite creators.

While looking at the data of conversation among users, the team found that many users on ShareChat were looking to showcase their work. Ankush says, 'People in smaller cities enjoy creating and sharing content as it gives them a sense of being creative.' By thinking on behalf of its users, ShareChat has created unexpected opportunities for people. For instance, Manoj from Uttar Pradesh always wanted to become a public speaker. Unfortunately, he had a minimal audience in his village, and because of financial limitations, his parents advised him not to think about becoming a speaker. He started recording his cricket commentary videos and posting them on ShareChat. Soon, he built a considerable fan base on the platform. Slowly, he became an online star, and as luck would have it, one day, he received a call from a Delhi-based media company, and landed a job in a Hindi video news company.

Many people are also using ShareChat to solicit business. For example, after completing his Class X, Narinder from Bhatinda joined a diploma course, but due to the poor financial situation of his family, he could not complete his studies and dropped out. He knew that he had to do something for his family, and for that, he needed to expand his small tailoring business. Through WhatsApp shares, he got to know about ShareChat, and he explored the platform. He thought that ShareChat could help him reach a vast audience. In his first post in May 2018, he shared his number so that people could contact him for embroidery designs. He got a lot of views on his post, and he started putting suit designs up regularly. Now he has around

400–450 customers on ShareChat who contact him for work. Astrologers, plumbers, tailors, carpenters, electricians and even a user who has manufactured a detergent powder at home promote their wares, posting their phone numbers and picking up orders through ShareChat.

The fashion stream on ShareChat has become a big hit with users as fashion in India is increasingly driven by small cities and towns. For instance, Shahana, a young entrepreneur from Malappuram, Kerala, sells clothes and fashion accessories on ShareChat. A homemaker who wanted to start a business from her home, Shahana initially tried Facebook and Instagram but did not receive much traction from these platforms, mainly because of the language barrier. When she heard about ShareChat, she believed that it would be the most comfortable platform for her to run a business. Now, she has over 16,000 followers on ShareChat and gets 90 per cent of her orders from the platform.

ShareChat has not only created business opportunities for its users, but it has also become a knowledge-sharing platform. For instance, Sopanraav started with traditional farming in Marathwada, a drought-prone area. He was interested in silkworm farming, and he travelled to Satara to learn silkworm farming techniques and returned to his village. Unfortunately, his first set of crops failed, but he tried again and, with his second effort, made a profit of ₹60,000. Around 2016, he used to see WhatsApp messages tagged with #agriinformation and decided to start a similar initiative on ShareChat. Today, he runs offline workshops, posts videos and pictures of his workshops, and shares tips on crop protection, silkworm farming and other related topics. Because of his popularity, people from Marathwada to Khandesh are in touch with him on ShareChat for queries regarding silkworm farming.

To connect the creators with their market, the company evolved the product further and assigned a dedicated team to mentor creators. By July 2019, ShareChat had more than 5,00,000 individual creators on its platform and a dedicated team that was mentoring 25,000 creators across 14 languages.

To bring forward a new generation of digital stars, in 2018, ShareChat collaborated with TVF (The Viral Fever) and launched a digital-first talent discovery platform called 'The Viral Stars'. This initiative has given millions of Indian youths across the country an opportunity to showcase their unique talents and become India's next generation of viral stars. ShareChat has also provided a platform to many regional celebrities and politicians to connect with their fans and followers. Moreover, it has created many micro-celebrities who now have over 3,00,000 followers on the platform. To sum up, ShareChat has empowered people to be creative, be productive and learn things they didn't think they could learn before. And as users benefit, they bring in more users through word of mouth.

Harness technology to understand and meet customer needs

Though technology works behind the scene, it plays a significant role in understanding users and providing them with a seamless experience. On the face of it, ShareChat looks simple. However, behind this simplicity is a high-tech architecture that is designed to handle scale and complexity, and also lend reliability to the product.

On ShareChat, millions of new posts are generated in the form of text, images and videos. With most vernacular language users coming online for the first time, and there being no precedent to their usage or their language, the nature of data and usage patterns being formed are varied, diverse and immense.

Moreover, internet behaviour varies within different ethnic groups, and first-time users differ by nature from long-time users. To analyse this kind of data and create valuable insights, the team puts in a lot of effort to train advanced Artificial Intelligence (AI) and Machine Learning (ML) algorithms in multiple languages. Data analysis allows the team to experiment simultaneously with numerous ideas and make decisions based on data rather than assumptions. It also helps in improving ideas that work and avoiding the ones that do not work.

With a massive amount of content posted, there is a fair amount of content that is replicated by users. To avoid issues like plagiarism and duplication of content, the team determines which piece of content was posted first, and groups it together with its duplicate on the platform. This, in turn, helps give credit to the original content creator. Plagiarism detection is not the only problem the team needs to address. Being the guardians of the platform, the team also needs to remove fake news and ethically and morally questionable content. The team applies stringent quality filters and fact-checkers, which ensure that fake news and propaganda do not spread on the platform. The team can easily track down the phone number of a user and even block the device. For instance, once the team took down 50,000 accounts that were posting objectionable content.

To provide scalability, reliability and performance, ShareChat runs its IT infrastructure through cloud-based technologies and runs a micro-service architecture with a vast number of internal and external services serving billions of requests daily. Also, to serve millions of users, the team has automated many processes through 120 tools built in-house. ShareChat deploys a set of algorithms that take into account about 40 signals to detect and report content. For example, anything pornographic is detected by the algorithms and deleted even before it goes live. Furthermore, the team has created several algorithms to serve personalised content, that is, the right content to the right users at the right time.

Along with creating features and checks for users, technology also helps the team deploy and test various monetisation models. So far, the team has experimented with 10–15 major monetisation models, like native advertising, micropayments, games and talent hunts on sets of 200–300 users. Although the company is focused on growth at the moment and has not finalised monetisation models, these experiments generate useful user insights on various monetisation models.

ShareChat is using technology to understand the expectations of vernacular language internet users and to create features to exceed these expectations. For instance, in May 2018, ShareChat launched the Shake-N-Chat feature, which allowed anonymous users to connect over a private chat. The matching algorithms take into account the content consumption patterns of the users and connects users with similar interests. Another example, to facilitate content sharing, ShareChat has provided a one-touch WhatsApp sharing option. At the same time, to maintain privacy, users can choose to disable WhatsApp sharing of their posts.

Build a great team

Steve Jobs said, 'Great things in business are never done by one person, they're done by a team of people.' Ankush, Bhanu and Farid have been working as a team since their college days. They have seen many failures and difficult days together, and they have developed a mutual understanding. During its initial years, investors like India Quotient, SAIF Partners and Lightspeed Venture Partners funded the company because they loved the energy, passion and chemistry of the team. Investors believed in the team and its ability to iterate, which is required to continuously upgrade a social media product. The initial rounds of funding helped the co-founders evolve the product and hire new team members. Over time, ShareChat scaled up and attracted more investors and team members.

Though all the co-founders are excellent programmers, they have their unique strengths, and they have divided their responsibilities accordingly. Ankush is the Chief Executive Officer, Farid is the Chief Operating Officer and Bhanu is the Chief Technology Officer. To develop the business side of the product, Sunil Kamath joined the team as Chief Business Officer in 2017. As ShareChat is solving many puzzles around regional languages and the behaviour of first-time internet users, it is very selective in its hiring process—it believes in hiring people who are good and fast with iterations, have a zest to solve problems and have empathy for internet users in vernacular languages.

Most of the hiring at ShareChat has happened through the network. Initially, out of 40 team members, 25 were from IIT Kanpur. They all had lucrative offers in hand or were working in well-known companies, but the ShareChat co-founders were able to inspire them to join their mission of shaping the experience of millions of Indians logging on to the internet for the first time. As many of the earlier team members had studied in Kanpur and were from tier-2 and tier-3 towns, they connected with the problem statement and the product's vision. In a few cases, when candidates were not convinced about joining the company, the co-founders suggested that they ask their parents in tier-2 and tier-3 towns about ShareChat, and interestingly, many people found ShareChat content in their family WhatsApp groups. Seeing their family members using the product, many candidates became interested in joining the team.

Farid says, 'We started right after college, and the people we started working with were also freshers or just had a year's experience, so that feeling of college was still present in them. In college, you have to do multiple things such as finish your homework, attend classes, pass your exams, and that kind of multitasking culture got extended here.' Whatever the team members are doing, whether it is fixing a bug or a small app release, they focus on getting things done. The team has put in significant effort in building ShareChat's technology architecture so that the product works smoothly even in areas with poor network, and every time a user logs in, the platform is working to serve them.

As the company continues to grow, it is becoming more and more essential to hire excellent people and keep them motivated. Interestingly, as vernacular social networking is an evolving concept, and many first-time internet users are joining the platform, the number of problem statements in the company is always more than the number of team members. Working on these first-time problems along with the feeling that they are working on ways to make ShareChat India's answer to global behemoths like Facebook, Instagram and Twitter keeps the team members motivated.

Since language is the mode of communication, it plays a vital role in sharing ideas, creating relationships, and increasing engagement within social networks. For a long time, English has dominated the internet. But now times are changing. Interestingly, India has overtaken America to become the world's second-largest base of internet users, and the next wave of users, including many regional language speakers, are coming online. Non-English-speaking users, however, are hesitant to enter social networks popular among English-speaking users, as they feel they will be judged for the kind of content they want to consume and share.

By eliminating English, ShareChat has possibly lost the top 15 million users who are active on social networks like Facebook, Twitter and Instagram in India. However, by bringing the power of social media to the bottom of the pyramid, it has created opportunities for vernacular language users to connect, communicate and collaborate in their own language with many other like-minded people. On ShareChat, the semi-urban and rural population does not get intimidated by the urban elite. Vernacular users can be themselves without being judged for their limited (or lack of) understanding of the English language. Undoubtedly, ShareChat is a beautiful example of how technology can be leveraged for social change.

Advice from Ankush Sachdeva

- Sometimes rejected ideas also become successful businesses in the long run. When nobody is considering your ideas, there will be lesser competition. So, don't ignore your ideas because of others' opinions.
- Successful innovation is not a single breakthrough. It is backed by many failures. Develop a high tolerance for failures. It takes a long time to find the right product for the right market.

ANKUSH SACHDEVA

- Sometimes your consumer segment can be very different from you and people with whom you work, like your investors and team members. In such a scenario, don't rely on assumptions. Remain singlemindedly focused on your consumer segment and validate your assumptions.
- New companies rarely have money to pour into advertising campaigns. Instead, they have to find creative ways to tap into existing networks to distribute their products. To get initial traction, we growth hacked by creating several WhatsApp groups where ShareChat content could be shared.

Helping people avoid the hassles of grocery shopping

The Bollywood movie *Mission Mangal* chronicles the story of India's Mars mission—Mangalyaan. This movie shows how India successfully sent a satellite to Mars on its first attempt. It is a classic story of the underdog, as, by the time Mangalyaan happened, America had failed to carry out a similar mission four times. Inspiringly, scientists Rakesh Dhawan (played by Akshay Kumar) and Tara Shinde (played by Vidya Balan), who had failed to send a GSLV satellite into space, architected this successful mission. The Mangalyaan is a textbook example that showcases that India doesn't always have to follow the Western world. Today, Mangalyaan is considered among the country's most crucial space achievements.

Like space missions, when people think of successful internet businesses, the first country that comes to their mind is America, which is the birthplace of global internet giants like Google,

Amazon, Facebook, among many others. Most of the internet businesses that started in India had a successful role model to look up to in America. But one successful internet business in India didn't have that luxury. Unfortunately, Webvan, the poster boy of America's dot-com bubble burst, was repeatedly used to define the bleak future of the online grocery business model. But today, this business model has become India's largest online grocery store—BigBasket.

Just like the comeback of the Mangalyaan team after their previous failure, the rise of BigBasket is a real comeback story. In 1999, a few entrepreneurs came together to start India's first online retail business FabMart.com. At that time, India wasn't quite ready for online shopping, and FabMart couldn't succeed. In 2011, these entrepreneurs came together again to create BigBasket. By 2019, BigBasket was present in 26 Indian cities, had over 12 million registered customers and was delivering over 55 million items every month and 1,50,000 orders per day.

From the outside, BigBasket might look like a grocery delivery company. But in the back end, its business is spread across procurement, supply chain, logistics and consumer services. It also owns multiple grocery brands such as Fresho, Royal, Tasties, Fresho Signature, Good Diet, BB Home and Happy Chef. BigBasket also runs an accelerator—BB Accelerate—which nurtures early-stage food and FMCG brands. Once these brands mature, they are handed over to their respective categories. By October 2019, BB Accelerate had nurtured over 25 brands.

BigBasket is considered one of the most valuable startups in India and has been backed by marquee investors like the World Bank's private-sector lending arm IFC, China's e-commerce giant Alibaba, CDC Group, which is a development financial institution owned by the UK government, South Korea-based private equity firm Mirae Asset, Helion Venture Partners,

Bessemer Venture Partners, Abraaj Group, LionRock Capital, Sands Capital, Ascent Capital, GrowthStory and Zodius Capital.

THE BEGINNING

Born and brought up in Mumbai, Hari Menon graduated from BITS Pilani in 1983 and worked with many renowned companies, including Wipro, PlanetAsia.com and TVS Electronics, where he got exposed to the internet. In 1999, he decided to start India's first e-commerce company FabMart. This was at a time when the internet used to run on slow dial-up connections, payment gateways were not available, the internet user base was minuscule, the Indian consumer was not comfortable making online transactions, and deliveries were difficult. The business model was too ahead of its time and the dot-com burst added to the injury.

Instead of continuing the online model via FabMart, the team decided to switch to the offline model and started a physical grocery chain by the name FabMall. In 2006, FabMall was acquired by the Aditya Birla Group and became a part of its retail brand—More. Post this exit, Hari started working as the CEO of Manipal City and Guilds, which provides skill development and vocational education.

In July 2011, during a casual conversation, serial entrepreneur and GrowthStory founder Krishnan Ganesh suggested that co-founders of FabMart and FabMall—Hari Menon, V.S. Sudhakar, Vipul Parekh and V.S. Ramesh—think about starting an online grocery business again. The team had already burnt their hands while trying to sell groceries online in 1999. In terms of age, the team members were in their forties and fifties and were pursuing different things in life. Moreover, investors had reservations about online grocery businesses because, when the dot-com bubble burst, an online grocery company, Webvan, had failed after a $1 billion cash burn. Over the years, many well-funded companies had tried selling groceries online, but hardly anyone had succeeded. The UK-based Ocado was an exception.

History has demonstrated that entrepreneurs discuss obstacles but also look for hidden opportunities. In 1999, FabMart couldn't succeed because the ecosystem was not ready. But 2011 was different. Broadband had picked up, payment gateways were present, smartphones were popular, and Flipkart was demonstrating serious traction in terms of online transactions. From an ecosystem-readiness perspective, the timing was right. Rather than being discouraged by the challenges of the online grocery business, the team felt motivated to solve the problems.

Eventually, in December 2011, Hari Menon, V.S. Sudhakar, Vipul Parekh and V.S. Ramesh joined hands with Krishnan Ganesh to start BigBasket. Meanwhile, Sudhakar and Vipul were advising Abhinay Choudhari on a similar online retail venture. They discussed this idea with him, and Abhinay also came on board.

THE BRAND NAME: BIGBASKET

The team's earlier ventures were called FabMart and FabMall, and they were interested in similar names for the new venture. FabBasket emerged as an option.

One day, Krishnan Ganesh walked in and asked the team, 'Why not BigBasket?' Everyone liked the name, as it was simple, easy to remember, and connected well with the nature of business. Hari immediately checked to see if the domain name was available and fortunately, they managed to buy the domain Bigbasket.com.

BUSINESS LESSONS

Many valuable lessons can be learnt from the evolution of BigBasket, a few of which follow.

Understand how to run your business well, before you scale-up

Steve Jobs said, 'Start small, think big. Don't worry about too many things at once. Take a handful of simple things to begin with, and then progress to more complex ones. Think about not just tomorrow, but the future. Put a ding in the universe.' The mindset of the BigBasket co-founders is a testament to this statement.

When the BigBasket co-founders started the business, they searched for a company that had been able to scale-up the online grocery business successfully. Fortunately, they found Ocado, a not-so-popular company based out of the UK. The team made the success metrics of Ocado its goals and decided to first achieve these metrics in one city. As all the co-founders were based in Bengaluru, they chose it as the first city of operation.

An online retail business has three sides to its operations. The first is the buying side, the second is the management of stocks in warehouses, and the third is delivery. Let's have a look at how BigBasket built its buying side.

Grocery can be divided into three sub-categories: dry groceries such as a pack of washing powder, chilled and frozen groceries such as ice cream, and fresh groceries such as fruits and vegetables. BigBasket started with an asset-light model. To fulfill dry grocery orders, the company tied up with India's leading business-to-business wholesaler METRO Cash & Carry and supermarket chain HyperCity. For fruits and vegetables, the company tied up with Safal, a large wholesale company of Mother Dairy.

From a stocking perspective, the company rented warehouses and transhipment hubs. A customer order that was to be delivered in the morning hours needed to be packed at a warehouse the previous evening and moved to a transhipment hub at night. It would stay there overnight and then be loaded into a van for delivery the next morning. Now, if the order included chilled and frozen items, like frozen peas, butter or ice cream, issues of damage could arise. These items would lie at the hub overnight inside insulation boxes without active refrigeration. Despite using the best insulation boxes, the heat ingress would sometimes damage the products. Unfortunately, there were many customer complaints regarding this category.

To meet customer expectations of fresh fruits and vegetables, for the first year, every morning at 3.30 a.m., the co-founders visited a righteous wholesale fruits and vegetables market to buy produce. Simultaneously, to solve the damage problem, the team tried to create an end-to-end cold chain. However, there were additional complexities: leafy vegetables needed to be stored at a temperature of 5 degrees Celsius, meat at -5 degrees Celsius and frozen items like ice cream and frozen meats at -25 degrees Celsius. The team worked hard to identify a solution to the problem of different temperatures. Eventually, they identified a gel that could freeze at these three different temperatures. This gel was packed into hard plastic cases and frozen in various types of freezers at the warehouse. The team worked with suppliers across the world to customise insulation box designs and got them manufactured in India and China.

The team also defined rules for better stock management at the warehouses. For example, fast-moving items got a slot close to pick-up locations so that they could be picked up and delivered quickly. To avoid traffic jams among pickers, two fast-moving items were placed slightly away from each other.

To prevent the toppling of the racks, heavy items were kept at the bottom of the racks. To keep eatables, like biscuits, away from hazardous items, like toilet cleaners, different sections were defined for hazardous and non-hazardous items. To avoid the mixing of products from the same brand, like Maggi chicken masala and Maggi vegetable atta noodles, even the same brand items were kept at a little distance. Similarly, every minute detail was defined to make sure that the warehouses ran efficiently.

For a capital-intensive, consumer-facing business like online grocery, logistics is the key to excellent customer experience. Initially, the company leased multiple vans to deliver orders. As the business grew, the number of transhipment hubs kept going up. Large trucks would move orders in bulk from warehouses to hubs where these orders would be unloaded, segregated, and reloaded into smaller vans for final dispatch to customers. Due to traffic, delivery via vans would take time. Moreover, vans were not cost-efficient for deliveries of small orders. To combat this, BigBasket created mini warehouses, called dark stores, near customer clusters. The dark stores hold lesser items as opposed to warehouses. The top-up and urgent orders were directly picked from the closest dark store and, instead of a van, a biker would take an order to the customer's doorstep.

The overall delivery experience depends on the behaviour of a delivery person, presentation of the products, and the ability of the delivery person to handle exceptional circumstances and complaints. Now, a single order could comprise of many different items. For instance, an order could have washing powder, meat, toilet cleaner, a broom, eggs, ice cream, and even some fragile items like a glass bottle. All of them need to be packed neatly and assembled thoughtfully so that the food items don't get mixed with the non-food items. The delivery personnel were trained to be patient while a customer checked their order. To avoid any conflict, the company operated on a no-questions-asked return policy. So, if a customer had any issue with any item in the order, the delivery personnel would take that item back. Also, the delivery personnel was not supposed to get in touch with a customer for any last-mile navigation or any other reason. Every delivery person was assisted by the delivery app and supported by a customer service agent.

After building the back end, including the sourcing process, stock management process, delivery network, technology infrastructure, and running the business successfully in Bengaluru, in October 2012, BigBasket was launched in Mumbai and Hyderabad. For the next two years, BigBasket operated only in these three cities. Around November 2013, BigBasket moved from an asset-light model that was dependent on METRO, HyperCity and Safal to an inventory-based model. This helped it in many ways. The company was able to offer same-day delivery with very high fill rates to the customers, and their margins also doubled.

By late 2014, BigBasket expanded to Chennai, Pune and Delhi NCR, with a warehouse in each city. It then expanded to Kolkata and Ahmedabad, and by the beginning of 2016, it had entered 17 tier-2 cities as well. In 2016, BigBasket introduced the Farmer Connect programme to procure fresh produce directly from farmers, thereby eliminating the middlemen.

Along with B2C, BigBasket also strengthened its B2B business by expanding to the HoReCa (Hotels, Restaurants and Caterers) segment. It is worth mentioning that BigBasket also started its private label brands, which now constitute 35 per cent of its revenue. The company serves its private labels to the HoReCa segment. It also sells numerous FMCG brands via over 10,000 neighbourhood stores in eight cities. Inspiringly, by

2018, BigBasket had expanded into 26 cities and had surpassed Ocado in many of its business metrics.

Look at everything from a customer's perspective

Grocery accounts for 50–60 per cent of the total retail market in India, which makes it the largest category. From local kirana stores to nearby supermarkets, customers have numerous options from where to purchase groceries. But traffic on roads, finding parking at a store and time spent in payment queues are big hassles for customers. So, from a convenience perspective, customers look up to online channels to buy groceries.

Now, you may be thinking what is so complex or unique about the online grocery business. To set the context, online grocery is a very different business from other online categories such as electronics and fashion. Unlike electronics or fashion, which are predominantly wants, grocery is a need. If the delivery of a mobile phone gets delayed by a day, customers can adjust. But if the delivery of fresh and needed groceries gets delayed, then a customer's whole day can get derailed. Also, unlike electronics and fashion, grocery is a low margin business.

Let us look at a few more complexities of this business. A customer orders a mobile phone maybe once a year and apparel four times a year. But grocery is ordered at least 36 times a year. So, a customer would experience the grocery brand a higher number of times than a fashion or electronics brand. Moreover, an electronics or fashion order is likely to contain one or two items. In contrast, a grocery order may have more than 20 items. To sum up, selling groceries online is a tough business. Numerous entrepreneurs across the world have tried selling groceries online, but there have been more failures than success stories.

In such a hard-to-crack category, the rise of BigBasket is inspirational. Hari says, 'Grocery is a consumer business, and in the consumer business, the single most important thing is the consumer experience.' Because of their experience of creating FabMall, the co-founders not only developed in-depth domain knowledge in retail but also developed the ability to empathise with consumers. They understand that the principal value proposition of online grocery is to provide convenience and avoid a visit to the offline store. Hence, since the start of the business, they follow the three golden metrics of grocery retail.

The first important metric is the fill rate, which is a measure of the extent to which a customer's order is fulfilled. For instance, if a customer ordered ten items, and the retailer delivered eight of them, then the fill rate was 80 per cent. Stocking inventory of perishable products without demand or delivering unstocked perishable items in a small window between the order and the delivery time are some of the fundamental challenges in providing a 100 per cent fill rate. If the fill rate is less than 100 per cent, then a retailer has not been able to fill that customer basket with everything that the customer needs, and the customer will go to an offline store to buy the remaining products. Providing the expected fill rate requires a deep understanding of inventory management, forecasting techniques, supply chain management and distribution partnerships. Interestingly, BigBasket has a fill rate of 99.5 per cent, which is considered the best in the industry from a customer delight perspective.

The second important metric is on-time delivery. If grocery doesn't come on time, then a mother might not be able to pack her children's tiffin on time, a family might miss their morning tea, no one may be available to receive a delayed order—the list can go on. In a nutshell, consumers are disappointed by unscheduled deliveries. They prefer a specific and predefined slot for delivery, chosen at the time of placing an order. Interestingly, BigBasket introduced a 100 per cent slotted delivery from day one. Moreover, it offers a delivery guarantee, which means that if an order delivery gets delayed, BigBasket will pay the customer 10 per cent of the order value.

The third essential metric is the in-stock rate, which means when a consumer comes to the store, the item that they are looking for should not be out of stock. The quantity and varieties a customer is looking for are increasing day by day. People of Indian origin returning from foreign countries are bringing in food habits cultivated there and are playing a significant role in influencing tastes and habits. Furthermore, TV and online programmes are creating awareness about products that were earlier unheard of.

Consumption of fruits like kiwi, dragon fruit and avocado as well as that of vegetables like lettuce is rising. Also, rare apple varieties like Fuji, Gala and Granny have become common now. Today, the range of chocolates and ice creams available is mind-boggling. The variety of cheese consumed now would shock anyone from the previous generation. Interestingly, there is a growing consumer segment that has a strong preference for organically grown food. Moreover, restaurants that specialise in global cuisines such as Indonesian, Vietnamese, Caribbean, Korean, French and Spanish are growing, and their purchasing departments also visits BigBasket to source raw materials and ingredients. Impressively, BigBasket has an out-of-stock experience of less than 4 to 5 per cent.

The team understood that if they couldn't maintain these numbers, BigBasket would soon end up as an undifferentiated business. But, if they cracked these three problems, it would be untouchable. For a business that delivers more than 2 million orders and more than 50 million items every month across 26 cities, planning is everything. Meeting a fill rate of 99.5 per cent, an on-time delivery rate of 99 per cent, and an in-stock experience of 95–96 per cent every day, day after day, is not easy. It may not be incorrect to say that, so far, no e-commerce company in India is close to achieving these operating metrics.

Steve Jobs said, 'I think if you do something and it turns out pretty good, then you should go do something else wonderful, not dwell on it for too long. Just figure out what's next.' Treading a similar path, the BigBasket team continuously looks for new ways to provide better consumer experience. For instance, BigBasket decided to offer chopped vegetables for sale, for the convenience of its customers. It has over 100 SKUs (stock-keeping units) for just cut vegetables now. Later, to promote healthy snacking, BigBasket started offering a ready-to-eat assortment of fruits, both in family and single-serve packs.

Customer experience is the centre of all processes at BigBasket. In case of any issues related to delivery, product quality and so on, customers can reach out to BigBasket through chat, email, phone and the company's social media channels. The company's goal is to connect a customer with a customer support agent within ten seconds, 98 per cent of the time. Customer support at BigBasket has a lot of other unique features. For example, an agent can see all customer interactions through various channels in a single interface. Furthermore, if a customer has more than two interactions on a complaint ticket, and the issue remains unresolved, the third interaction is handled by a senior customer support executive. In case customers have given a lower rating for any order, then the customer support team calls the customer to understand the issue.

Hari says, 'Nowadays, customers don't complain much, maybe they are happy or like to give a second chance or switch over to substitutes. If they come forward to complain, it means they are allowing us to improve. We take every complaint seriously and constantly push ourselves to provide a better customer experience.'

Disrupt your own business

John Chambers said, 'If you don't innovate fast, disrupt your industry, disrupt yourself, you'll be left behind.' Over time, more and more companies have started entering the online grocery business. Moreover, customers have been using neighbourhood kirana stores and supermarkets for decades. In a crowded and competitive market, customer satisfaction is the only key distinguisher. A dissatisfied customer will quickly switch to other players, which has a direct impact on business and revenue. Though BigBasket has emerged as a leader in the online retail business, it continually works on customer-centric innovations to remain ahead of the curve. Let us look at a few examples that demonstrate BigBasket's laser-sharp focus on customer satisfaction.

BigBasket started with an asset-light model. In this model, the company accepted orders on its app and website, collected items from wholesalers like METRO Cash & Carry and HyperCity, and delivered them. The company didn't have the cost of holding inventory in its warehouses, but it operated on wafer-thin margins as wholesalers took their shares from the margins provided by the manufacturer. Apart from lower margins, the company had less control over product quality, variety and availability. So, BigBasket moved its business from the asset-light to the inventory-based model. In the inventory model, money is spent on warehouses and inventory holding, but the business extracts significantly higher margins as it buys directly from brands and manufacturers.

A consumer buys groceries in three ways: planned buying, top-up buying and specialty buying. At the beginning or towards the end of the month, customers buy some items. These items are not required urgently. These kind of purchases form the planned buys. Beyond planned, a consumer buys certain things every week, such as fruits, vegetables, bread, dairy and eggs. The shelf life of these items is short, and customers need them fast. This forms the top-up buying. And then there is specialty buying; for instance, Karachi Bakery's biscuits in Hyderabad or bread from Bengaluru's Iyengar Bakery. Typically, the spending on groceries by any household comprises 60–65 per cent of planned buying, 20–25 per cent of weekly top-up buying, and the remaining speciality store buying.

For planned deliveries, the inventory-led model was working fine, and for weekly top-up buying, BigBasket wanted to tap into the kirana-store network and share its technology with them. The company had planned to sign up kirana stores to maintain a small assortment of around 200–400 products that customers might need urgently. But then the team realised that this plan may result in a disappointing experience. Not every store was professionally run—they kept different timings, and many stores found it challenging to follow systems and technology. Moreover, helpers at these stores quit frequently, and it was a pain to train the new recruits constantly. The company couldn't have delivered a consistent experience and knew that it could not scale-up this way. So, this plan was dropped.

To solve the problem of urgent deliveries, the company opened dark stores, which are mini warehouses near residential areas that are not open to the public. These stores hold inventory of fast-moving or urgently required items. Also, to add a fleet of bikes for delivery, the company acquired logistics startup Delyver. This move accelerated the shift to 'express delivery' in

90 minutes. Furthermore, to foray into the micro-delivery of milk and other daily essentials before 8 a.m., BigBasket acquired delivery startups RainCan and Morning Cart and branded the service as BB Daily. BB Daily is a subscription service that allows customers to order daily essentials like milk the previous night and have them delivered the following morning. To provide fresh products twenty-four seven, BigBasket acquired a smart vending machines startup, called Kwik24, and branded the service BB Instant. The unmanned vending machines are installed in apartments and office complexes. Customers can take fresh produce and other FMCG products from these vending machines using the BB Instant app. It involves human intervention only for restocking.

While BigBasket was expanding to various cities and adopting multiple delivery models, the biggest challenge that it faced was to serve the customers in the time span promised. Another issue that the team faced was the small window between the order and the delivery time. Very short planning time for shipments is tough to manage using the manual planning processes. To cope with these challenges, BigBasket partnered with Locus, an AI-based decision-making platform for the supply chain.

Locus helps BigBasket in automating its route planning process and optimising operations. It creates comprehensive route plans that are data-driven and not intuition-based. Most orders are routed in a way that customer expectations are met. Locus also suggests the best fleet combination to enhance capacity utilisation based on historical traffic data, weight and volumes parameters, customer time slot preference, and other business constraints. Moreover, the solution also includes real-time re-routing using an interactive and intuitive dashboard.

As customers shop from BigBasket to save time, the company created a goal to get regular customers to check out in two to three minutes. To create the fastest possible shopping experience on-site, the company built a solution called Smart Basket. It populates a customer's basket based on their most recent and frequent purchases, alerts them if they have not added something they usually buy and informs them if an item they usually buy is about to run out. After a customer has placed about ten orders or so, Smart Basket will start recommending items to the customer. These recommendations are based on the order history of the customer, how similar kinds of customers buy, and what the customer is likely to buy. Therefore, the idea is that if customers use Smart Basket, they should be able to pick 80–90 per cent of the items in just a couple of minutes. This makes shopping convenient for customers, and they get hooked on to the online grocery buying experience.

Beyond these examples, there is a long list of innovations. Hari says, 'We were clear that we wanted to build a company that is extremely strong on processes. This is a very execution-focused business, and to have high-class execution, process and technology have to be the base of everything we do and would do.'

Combine marketing with the power of analytics

Initially, BigBasket's focus was on building online grocery as a category and persuading customers that BigBasket is a brand worth trying. So, the messaging was primarily about convenience and trust. Since in the first few years, BigBasket's operations were limited to a few cities, the company focused on below-the-line (BTL) activities in malls and apartments besides poster and banner campaigns, radio ads and some print ads in local newspapers. From a digital marketing perspective, the company focused on targeted advertising through Facebook, Google

AdWords (SEM), SEO and affiliate marketing. This activation started bringing people to the website.

When people used BigBasket, they found that not only was it convenient and time-saving, it offered great variety and lower prices compared to neighbourhood stores. On-time delivery of orders, a no-questions-asked return policy, good quality of delivered items, and assistance provided in solving complaints helped in establishing BigBasket as a reliable platform. Soon people started talking about the service with their neighbours, and word of mouth started picking up. The company painted its delivery vans with the brand logo and messages focused on its value proposition. These vans acted as zero-cost moving billboards within the city, and people started noticing BigBasket's service in action.

By 2015, BigBasket had entered multiple cities. Hence, there was a need to create brand awareness at a large scale. The company decided to get a brand ambassador on board. Because of his universal appeal that cuts across age, gender and geography, Shah Rukh Khan (SRK) appeared as the preferred choice. SRK is also known for his professionalism and dedication to work, so his professional traits also matched with the traits of BigBasket. With him on board, the company started mass awareness campaigns through media like TV ads.

Since BigBasket was using multiple marketing channels, it became essential to track which channel were bringing in customers, what kind of acquisition cost BigBasket was paying for each new customer, and what the eventual retention of each customer onboarded via a particular channel was. An analysis of channel performance data helped the team figure out which channels were the best and, accordingly, optimise the marketing mix by channel. The BigBasket team analysed the performance of various channels, including TV campaigns. The team knew at what time the brand's advertisements were getting released and on which channel. Keeping a lag of about three seconds after an ad was released, they checked for customer visits and conversions.

As a result of a thorough analysis, the team could correlate which channels and which insertions were working well for the brand. Over a period, the team realised which channel gave better conversions and at what time of the day. The team was able to streamline the entire marketing campaign and reduce marketing costs by about 30–40 per cent, while getting the same number of visits and conversions.

Moreover, SRK's endorsement helped immensely with the brand's visibility. As the number of customers transacting on BigBasket started increasing, the team started tracking the behaviour of loyal and new customers. They also looked at the behaviour of customers who were on the verge of becoming loyal. Through this exercise, the team learnt about the kind of items different types of customers buy, how often they visit, and what pages they visit. Soon, the team started using this analysis to customise its offerings to customers. The idea was to tune offerings based on what stage a customer was in their lifecycle with BigBasket. For example, for new customers, the site would show more offers than it would for regular customers. For the regular customer, the site would be customised to show more categories, such that they buy a larger variety of products.

Beyond marketing, social media is also becoming a customer service channel for BigBasket. The company has built a dedicated team to address users' queries and concerns on social media. The team has also set strong KPIs (key performance indicators); for instance, a Facebook post needs to be responded to within three minutes, a tweet needs to be answered in five minutes, a comment on the Play Store has to be answered in 30 minutes and so on.

The team monitors how many posts are responded to within the stipulated time, how many posts were repeated, and how many interactions did it take to resolve a particular complaint. Ideally, the idea is to solve everything in one communication. So, if some query has multiple interactions, it means that the customer service is not working well. The team uses that experience to figure out how to react better and provide better customer service.

By keeping one foot in marketing and the other in analytics, BigBasket has been able to seize relationship-building and growth opportunities quickly. Moreover, it has been able to adapt its product to meet the customers' needs.

Take care of your employees and suppliers

Herb Kelleher said, 'Your employees come first. And if you treat your employees right, guess what? Your customers come back, and that makes your shareholders happy. Start with employees, and the rest follow from that.'

BigBasket has over 23,000 employees, 75 per cent of them are blue-collared employees, including packers, stackers and delivery boys. They are expected to come to their respective offices at 6.30 a.m. and deliver at 7 a.m. with a smile. If on any day, 30 people don't turn up, the company can't deliver the products with ease that morning. Hari says, 'From our warehouse to our last-mile delivery, BigBasket is a very operationally intensive business, and we need to be sure that employees at all levels are motivated.'

A large number of new recruits come from rural India. Many times, they get so overwhelmed by the processes, workload and the work environment that they can't cope, and leave. To support the newcomers, the company has started a programme called Neev, in which top-performing seniors, called Team Leads, handhold the new employees for 60 days and get them up to speed. To keep the motivation levels of Team Leads high, they are incentivised with several benefits. Apart from Neev, the company has several other training programmes for its employees.

From a rewards and recognition perspective, the associates that form the top 20 per cent in each region are recognised every month and rewarded for their performance, and the bottom 20 per cent are sent for re-training. The company also has a bi-annual award called 'BB Rockstar', which is given to the top 30 associates across the country. BB Rockstars are flown to the corporate office in Bengaluru to attend the Annual Day, where they are called onto the stage amidst thunderous applause. Interestingly, even the families of Rockstars are invited to the award event. BigBasket also runs a trust for the blue-collar workforce. Any associate who has spent more than 12 months at the company is eligible for educational assistance (reimbursement for school and college fees, textbooks, etc.) for themselves and their families. Through the trust, the company has also tied up with expert organisations like LabourNet, which helps associates identify the right vocational courses that would enhance their employability and create jobs for their dependents.

Many blue-collar workers in large cities such as Bengaluru and Delhi are from northern and eastern states who have migrated from villages in search of work. For such migrants, clean drinking water, safety and hygiene are of foremost importance. For them, the company provides dormitory-style accommodation and shared apartments. Hari says, 'Shared housing brings down costs by at least 50 per cent, especially when done at scale. Also, it helps in retaining employees as well as making them more productive.'

On peak days, when the order flow is high, there is some stress at all levels. The pressure gets passed down and is manifested in rude behaviour and foul language. Sometimes, supervisors even turn down legitimate leave requests. This encourages associates to abscond without even the slightest intimation. The company has conducted training for supervisors and has automated the process around leaves, where denial of leave has to be approved by the function head. In cases where the team doesn't have the staff up to full capacity, they have to hold back, push orders, and talk to customers. Festival times are the most challenging. During this time, BigBasket increases the time for servicing any order, due to a huge rise in orders. So, when a customer places an order, they get a time slot for two days later. Hari says, 'Customers don't wait for two days for groceries. It is certainly a big negative, and we are grappling with it.'

Like its employees, BigBasket considers its suppliers as an extended family. To strengthen its backend for fresh produce, the company runs a farmer supply chain programme called Farmer Connect. The company has set up collection centres in rural areas to source vegetables from farms. BigBasket buys only from farmers registered with it. That's different from the opportunism of buying from the farmer offering the best price. It builds relationships with farmers by offering price transparency and direct payment into their bank accounts. In return, the company gets assured supply and quality.

Hari says, 'We have two commitments to the farming community. One, we help them get larger revenue as they sell directly to BigBasket, and the need for intermediaries is eliminated. Second, their payment is expedited, and they are paid within two days and that too directly into their bank accounts. Farmers appreciate this. Furthermore, we have agronomists in collection centres who advise farmers in terms of how to boost their yields, the right use of fertilizers, etc.' By October 2019, BigBasket had set up 40 collection centres around the country and was sourcing 80 per cent of its farm products directly from 10,000 farmers.

The company has also set processes for the convenience of suppliers who deliver items at its warehouses. Earlier, the supplier vehicles used to arrive at the warehouse at any time of the day. This resulted in chaos at the warehouse and a long waiting time for suppliers. Now, suppliers are provided with scheduled slots for delivery. A fast-track receiving mechanism is set for small vendors to complete receiving in 60 minutes. This allows small vendors to use their vehicles for other deliveries. For large vendors, receiving is completed within three hours. Also, the company has set up a waiting area for vendor teams to relax until the receiving process is complete. Hari says, 'A small difference made to the lives of many people comes back as great support from them. We aspire to become the most preferred employer for blue-collar workers, the most preferred partner for farmers and suppliers, and the most preferred retailer for customers.'

When BigBasket's team started their business many people said, 'If Webvan couldn't do it, how the hell will you do it?' Many investors rejected their business idea by saying, 'Nobody has cracked it in a big way. Why will you succeed in India when the people in the USA couldn't do it?' But on the lines of this famous saying of Michael Jordan's, 'Some people want it to happen, some wish it would happen, others make it happen', the BigBasket team made it happen.

HARI MENON

Advice from Hari Menon

- Customer experience is the core of brand building. So, focus on the experience. Always talk to customers, take their feedback, and understand what they like and dislike. Accordingly, try to create a better experience.
- Without capital, you cannot run a business. Raise sufficient money for the long run. Taking capital for a shorter period doesn't take you anywhere, as your focus gets divided between raising capital and running the business.
- Don't scale-up just because you have money. Along with capital, a business needs an ecosystem and a trustworthy founding team. So, think about scaling up when these fundamentals are in place.

HIDESIGN
Handcrafted. Since 1978.

Spreading India's craftsmanship globally

The word 'luxury' brings up thoughts of money and status, but the concept of luxury has a deeper meaning. Luxury products are a manifestation of the values, the culture and the skills of the craftsmen who create them. Indian craftsmen are recognised globally for their unmatched expertise in embroidery, jewellery design, leather work and weaving (with silk and pashmina wool).

But when people think about luxury brands, countries like France and Italy appear in their minds. Rarely does the name of India come up as a first thought. Why does this happen?

Is it because no luxury brands have emerged out of India, or because not many people know about them? Or maybe because people admire brands from other countries so much that they don't notice the accomplishments of Indian brands.

This was not always the perception. History tells us that pre-British India enjoyed a worldwide market for its manufactured products, and India's excellent level of craftsmanship was held in high regard. Sadly, colonial rule broke the backbone of the Indian handicraft industry. India's craftsmanship fell prey to rapid industrialisation, and our beloved country was reduced to being a supplier of raw materials.

However, the good news is that after Independence, a few Indian luxury brands have made their mark internationally. This is the story of one such brand—Hidesign. Interestingly, not many Indians know that Hidesign is an Indian brand.

Founded in 1978 as a small leather bags workshop in Puducherry, Hidesign has evolved to become a lifestyle brand with products ranging from bags and shoes to sunglasses and other luxury products. It is sold in 24 countries, including India, the USA, the UK, Australia, Kenya, UAE, Spain, Portugal, New Zealand and Sri Lanka. Along with leather products, the Hidesign group also runs two luxury boutique hotels in Puducherry—Le Dupleix and The Promenade.

Icons, celebrities, executives and models all over the world have a penchant for Hidesign products. Even dignitaries like Princess Diana, Hollywood filmmaker Steven Spielberg, former Prime Minister of India Indira Gandhi, Infosys founder Narayana Murthy, former President of South Africa Nelson Mandela, and many other eminent personalities have used Hidesign products. Inspiringly, in 2007, the world's most valuable luxury brand—Louis Vuitton—invested in Hidesign.

THE BEGINNING

The soul behind this soulful endeavour, Dilip Kapur was born in New Delhi. When he was nearly six years old, Dilip's spiritually inclined father sold his shoe business and came to the Sri Aurobindo Ashram in Puducherry. Dilip studied in the school in the Ashram and loved the liberal, unregimented atmosphere there. In 1963, at the age of 15, he came across a *Time* magazine article about the Phillips Academy in Andover, the oldest incorporated academy in the US. He didn't have the money to pay for his application, but he wrote a letter to the headmaster of the academy. Miraculously, the school offered him a full scholarship. In 1964, with just $8 in his pocket, Dilip landed in America.

After the Phillips Academy, he studied International Affairs at Princeton University and then did his PhD at the University of Denver. While in the US, he took up various jobs to sustain himself, which included working as a dishwasher and a waiter. During one of the summers, he applied for a job at a Denver-based leather factory called Poor Richard's. This nine-month stint resurrected his love for leather which had been in his blood all along. His father's leather shoe factory had been burnt down in the communal riots during the partition of India. He had never seen his father work with leather. But he learnt that he loved working with leather, dying it by hand, cutting it and assembling bags.

One day, while paying bills at the factory in Denver, Dilip noticed that all the rare leather imported from England was called E.I. Leather. Expensive shoes and bags were made from it. Out of curiosity, he searched and found out that E.I. stood for East India and was described as the most beautiful vegetable tanned leather in the world. To his surprise, the genesis of East India Leather had been some 150 km from his house in Puducherry.

When Dilip was in America, a vast cultural revolution against America's war on Vietnam was taking place. It was mainly powered by students, who were disgusted by the agony brought on by the war. As a student of international affairs at a prestigious university on the East Coast, Dilip witnessed the revolution at close quarters and became actively involved in the protests with his classmates. He founded a chapter of the Third World Liberation Front. Dilip had great admiration for America, the country had given him a lot over the last 15 years, but he didn't want to stay there anymore.

In the 1960s, the migration wave of Indians going to the West had not yet gained speed, and Dilip remembers being the only Indian at the Phillips Academy. In 1977, at the age of 30, he returned to India. It was shocking, as no Indian who went to America at that time wanted to come back. But Dilip did not connect with the mainstream, he didn't want a high-flying job. Rather than running after success, he was more interested in doing something experimental and challenging. On his visits during summer breaks, Dilip had seen the energy that had gone into the creation of Auroville. The idealist, hippie rebel in him really wanted to be a part of this vision of a new world. He volunteered to help develop Auroville, an experimental township established in 1968 near Puducherry, where much emphasis was placed on the goodness of nature and the vision that Sri Aurobindo cultivated.

Along with planting trees and planning the affairs of Auroville, Dilip taught international relations at Auroville's school. Meanwhile, he indulged in his hobby of designing leather bags. In his free time, he tried making bags with zero knowledge of design or fashion, which is probably what made his bags stand out.

He tied up with the local tanners and started working with leather, creating designs of his own. The first few bags he designed and made were gifted to his mother, sister and aunt. Once a generous and rich friend offered a handsome amount for a bag Dilip had designed. Dilip was surprised as he never expected someone to pay money and buy what he had made. He realised that what was a hobby could become his profession. In 1978, he started a small workshop with a capital of ₹25,000 and one cobbler.

Dilip's rugged, simple bags were radical in the 1970s. People visiting Auroville, from all over the world, started liking his products and took his bags to Germany, England, the USA, Australia and other countries. For two decades, after it was founded, Hidesign sold primarily to international markets. It started focusing on India as a potential market only in the year 2000.

THE BRAND NAME: HIDESIGN

A brand name should be easy to pronounce and should have a a rationale behind it. Sometimes, an ingredient of the product is brought into the spotlight in the brand name, as the image of the ingredient can have a positive influence on the consumer.

As Dilip was creating beautifully designed bags using hide (leather), he named the brand Hide Design. In this name, the term 'hide' represented the primary raw material, and the word 'design' represented the core attribute of the products.

In 1981, a London-based PR agency recommended a shorter single word for the brand name. According to them, Hide Design sounded a bit awkward because of the repetition of 'de'. The agency suggested to Dilip that the brand name should be simple and sound a bit serious. Based on this suggestion, Dilip merged the 'de' in the words 'hide' and 'design', and the brand name Hidesign was born.

BUSINESS LESSONS

Many important business lessons can be learnt from the evolution of Hidesign. A few of them follow.

Challenge the conventional

During the 1960s and 1970s, when Dilip was in America, the hippie subculture had begun as a youth movement. Hippies kept their hair long, experimented with new styles of clothing and music, and rebelled against the artificialness of mainstream society. Dilip had also joined the movement and become a radical. And with that philosophy in mind, despite having a PhD, Dilip left all the opportunities in America and started living in a hut in Puducherry.

From the beginning of his entrepreneurial journey, Dilip had been very ideological. Rather than selling, he was interested in creating products that could represent the rebel in him. Dilip says, 'I learnt from the cobbler Murugan, who was the first person to join Hidesign. Murugan taught me the art of working with leather, a skill he had inherited over generations. He was the most famous cobbler in Puducherry, an illiterate artist who could create beautiful patterns, a perfectionist who knew every aspect of leather work. In return for his knowledge, I sat with Murugan and taught him how the Italians hand colour leather, how a bag is constructed and never just stitched together, and the importance of the fall of a bag so that it looks gorgeous on a woman's arm.'

The hippies and a generation of people like Dilip that came out of the American cultural revolution were in love with things in their natural forms. In the 1970s, most of the leather sold in India was plasticky and artificial. Indian consumers preferred perfectly designed shiny and glossy leather bags, whereas Dilip's bags were very different from the mainstream. They had a rugged natural look because that's what Dilip believed in. Leather is a natural material with imperfections, and he considered these imperfections beautiful. Most Indians saw these imperfections as defects and couldn't relate to his products.

Steve Jobs once said, 'Believing that the dots will connect down the road will give you the confidence to follow your heart.'

Though many people criticised his creations, the rebel inside Dilip pushed him to follow his heart. Once, Dilip was selling a few of his bags in Auroville when Bernd Dreesman, a German visitor affiliated with a German organisation that campaigned for the eradication of world hunger, spotted his creations. He loved what he saw and ordered 1,400 bags. Dilip and his one worker failed to fulfil the order and delivered only 200. But the orders kept coming.

His second order was from Australia, where his bags were sold at hippie shops in Melbourne. Cow John, who managed cows in Auroville, had gone back to Australia to work in a car factory. When he broke his back, he got $12,000 from his company. With that money, he returned to Auroville, bought Dilip's bags, and sold them in Australia. He was quite successful in selling them. That was how Hidesign reached Australia.

With profits and advances from those first few buyers, Dilip added ten more workers and expanded his workshop to a separate house in Puducherry. One of the cousins of this Australian buyer was living in England. She saw Dilip's bags and was impressed. She started buying them for the UK market. Then, somebody who visited Auroville from California saw the bags and began selling them there. Because of the time he spent in America, Dilip's design sensibility was American. That helped his bags work well in the Western market.

The fashion world of the 1980s was full of pedigreed Italian and French bags. At that time, Hidesign was establishing itself as a unique hybrid brand. On the one hand, Dilip was relying on craftsmanship from the Indian cobbler caste, and using brass casting and traditional East India leather. On the other hand, Hidesign's cultural identity was clearly linked to the cultural revolutions that had swept through the Western world in the 1960s.

Dilip's products were very different from the mainstream bags sold in the international markets back then. The earthiness of natural leather and brass went well with the rebels rather than the mainstream population. Instead of mainstream stores, his bags started becoming popular in alternative stores that specialised in men's fashion and were targeting hippies and rebels. In 1985, one of the purchase managers of John Lewis & Partners, a chain of high-end departmental stores across the UK, used a Hidesign bag and liked it very much. He felt, if he liked the product, his customers would also like it. As luck would have it, the first significant purchase offer came from John Lewis & Partners. When people saw Hidesign products at John Lewis & Partners in London, the brand gained visibility among mainstream customers. In no time, young business executives were carrying Hidesign bags.

Followed by John Lewis, Hidesign started getting sold in high-end departmental stores like Selfridges, House of Fraser and Debenhams in Europe, and David Jones and Myers in Australia. The 1980s saw Hidesign become a cult brand among the highly fashionable customers of Castro Street and Haight-Ashbury in San Francisco, Portobello Road in London, and the alternative stores in Melbourne.

By the early 1990s, over 700 individual stores in London were selling Hidesign bags, which was a big deal for an Indian company. In 1992, Hidesign's Boxy Bag, a small bag made like an old-style suitcase with a long strap on it, was selected by *Accessory* magazine in the UK as the accessory of the year. Princess Diana presented the award, and this honour helped Hidesign reaffirm its position as a leading leather brand. In the late 1990s, the company started looking towards new markets, and developing economies such as South Africa, Russia, India and South East Asia. In 1997, Hidesign opened its first exclusive showroom in Moscow, Russia. In 1998, the brand entered the emerging markets of Malaysia, South Africa and China.

In the 1990s, the opening of the Indian economy saw hundreds and thousands of Indians going to study, trade and shop in the West. The income of Indians rose, and the growing middle class became more fashion-conscious. Indian consumers discovered Hidesign products while travelling abroad and bought them. Looking at the demand from NRIs and travellers, Hidesign started selling within India in 1999. Unlike foreign distributors, Indian distributors didn't relate to the brand, so the company decided to open its own stores. The first store was opened in Puducherry, followed by a store in Bengaluru.

Until 2000, 92 per cent of Hidesign products were sold abroad. Interestingly, in 2009, India surpassed the UK to become Hidesign's largest market. By November 2019, Hidesign had close to 100 exclusive stores in India across major airports and malls and sold through leading retail stores like Shoppers Stop, Lifestyle and Central, and major e-commerce websites such as Amazon and Flipkart. Internationally, the brand was present in 24 countries with over 2,000 stores and counted amongst the few Indian luxury brands that have made their mark globally.

You can't be everything to everyone

Luxury brands have a reputation for being elite, which adds to their perceived value. They differentiate themselves from mass brands by creating the perception of exclusivity. Perceptions of exclusivity can appear in terms of unattainable prices, limited geographic availability, brand heritage, high quality, communication or even barriers to possession. Luxury brands should not be accessible for everyone. At the same time, they must find customers who can afford and appreciate what these brands present.

Hidesign differs from other elite products as it is positioned as an affordable luxury brand. Its ideal customers include the well-informed, career-oriented, cosmopolitan people who appreciate well-made, handcrafted products and are sensitive to ecological issues. Executives were the first to buy Hidesign products. Models, advertising people, actresses, people going overseas followed soon. Over time, with rising income levels, aspirations of people in the service industry started growing, and they have also started looking at Hidesign products with keen interest.

What sets luxury brands apart from others is their reputation for quality and craftsmanship.They are often known for the time, effort, care and detail they put into their products, especially if they are handmade. In a sea of leather accessories brands, its styling, leather and merchandise set Hidesign apart from others. It has always focused on creating original designs. Today, the company has design teams based in London and Puducherry that work together to develop innovative cult designs. Its multicultural design team has won several international awards for its excellence and design leadership.

India used to be a prominent centre of vegetable-tanned leather, and the other two such centres in the world were Italy and Brazil. But when chemical tanning came to India, vegetable tanning vanished. Dilip always believed in sustainability and healthy living. He learnt about East India leather while interning in America, and on his return to India, he began researching it further. It is this mindset that attracted him to Auroville. He could not think of polluting nature with chemicals. So, he kept experimenting with vegetable-tanned leather and learning more about it.

By learning from the age-old skill of tanning leather with natural seeds and barks, Hidesign has created fashionable leathers that age exceptionally well. The art consists of soaking leather for 40 days in wattle bark and myrobalan seeds and then rubbing the tanned leathers with pungam oil, a native oil that makes the leather supple. This process gives the leather a rich, nourished look and feel, and tremendous strength and durability. Hidesign's leather is not corrected to hide defects with colour or pigments to cover the leather's natural beauty. The feel, look and smell of Hidesign's leathers are sensuous and natural. Apart from the leather, Dilip is equally stringent about the dyes used by them. Hidesign bags, which are known for their earthy hues and natural finish, are made with Azo-free dyes. Azo is a potential carcinogen; on the other hand, the dyes used by Hidesign are certified by the European community. Furthermore, the leathers are individually hand-coloured with a brush and polished with wax.

When faced with the choice of using either zinc alloy or steel buckles that have been electroplated to resemble brass, Hidesign decided to rediscover the art of brass buckles through the master craftsmen in Indian temple towns. In almost every home in India, there is a small corner devoted to a temple, and every temple has a brass sculpture of a god. Craftsmen in the small by-lanes of old towns spend hours creating these sculptures and sand-casting idols from molten brass. While brass is the preferred metal for many Indian gods, it is rarely used for buckles and bag fittings. Though the job of individually polishing a brass buckle is too complicated, time-consuming and expensive, the brass buckles on the Hidesign bags are sand-casted and polished painstakingly by hand. Hidesign does not have a mass manufacturing or assembly line system. Each bag is individually handcrafted by a team of three to six artisans. When it is time to stitch the bag, a group of well-trained craftsmen use their hands to sew the pieces together, and cutters cut leather with fine pointed knives—a skill that takes two years to master. With an average work experience of over 17 years, Hidesign has one of the most skilled teams of craftsmen in the leather goods industry worldwide.

Dilip says, 'A Hidesign bag is never made, it is "constructed". A handcrafted product, lovingly produced by a master, has a distinction, individuality, and soul—all essential to a feeling of personal luxury. This is what makes a Hidesign bag unique as compared to the other China bags available by the dozen.' All Hidesign bags are manufactured in-house. The company has four factory units—one in Sikkim, two in Puducherry, and a vegetable tanning unit in Ranipet. By October 2019, Hidesign was producing around 18,000 bags (for both men and women) and approximately 25,000 pieces of accessories per month. With the rapid expansion of Hidesign stores across India, its production capacity continuously remained stretched to its limits.

Dilip says, 'A luxury brand is created by narrowing the focus. If you focus on everyone, you lose your identity. A brand is all about having an identity.' Hidesign's focus on its customers, manufacturing process, and store experiences have helped it create a unique identity. Because of this unique identity, people talk about the brand, journalists write about it, and this word of mouth helps make it popular.

Development is born from objection

For almost two decades, Hidesign grew internationally through distributors. They liked Hidesign's products and placed them in the right stores. Fortunately, there was business growth, but, unfortunately, there was no direct connection with customers. Once, when a large distributor was acquired by a private equity player, Hidesign, suddenly lost a channel to almost 800 stores and their customers. That is something a person with artistic inclination doesn't want after creating a market. Though Dilip understood the challenges of dependency on distributors, he didn't have the bandwidth to reach out to retailers and customers in international markets directly.

In the year 2000, when Dilip decided to expand his business in India, he approached distributors. But Indian distributors had been used to selling goods that worked in India. They didn't connect with Hidesign's vision and had doubts about its products. Now, the only option left for Dilip was to open exclusive Hidesign stores. He had to develop a new capability of opening and operating his own stores.

Richard Branson said, 'If you spot an opportunity and are really excited by it, throw yourself into it with everything you've got.' Starting with its first store in Puducherry, by November 2019, Hidesign had close to 100 exclusive stores in India. Dilip has been very selective about the locations of these stores. He says, 'Your stores have to be where your customers are.' Initially, Hidesign focused on NRIs and foreigners. It opened stores wherever these people were present, like high-end malls, airports, tourist destinations like Goa and business centres like Delhi and Mumbai. They avoided main streets because they lacked the infrastructure and could not provide a shopping experience. So, the company eventually avoided opening stores in crowded and not-so-fashionable places.

As the aspiration and income levels of Indian consumers started rising, the profiles of Hidesign's customers also started expanding. The good part of having its own stores was the direct connection that Hidesign established with its customers. Appreciation and feedback started coming in, which were not present in the distributor-led model. In fact, Dilip had never thought about Hidesign as a brand; rather for him, it was just a name. But these retail stores and customer interactions made him realise that Hidesign was a brand that people admired.

When Louis Vuitton invested in the company, Dilip received the advice that a brand must be strong in its home country. So, he started focusing more on the Indian market, and soon, it became the largest market for Hidesign. All Hidesign stores are custom-designed using high-quality materials that are natural: solid brass, real leather and wood. The team at Hidesign nurtures a passion for design and thrives on shaping each store with a unique atmosphere, which is luxurious, warm and personal. Moreover, Hidesign's popularity in the West also played an important role in giving it recognition in India.

Along with its own exclusive stores, Hidesign also sells through 160 premium multi-brand retail stores in India. Within these stores, the brand designs its own sub-stores, which are controlled spaces that create brand experiences and communicate brand beliefs. Dilip says, 'One of the elements of brand building is recognition. Multi-brand retail stores bring the brand in touch with a wider audience. But along with this advantage, brand dilution also happens as it is difficult to replicate the exclusive store experience at multi-brand stores.'

Furthermore, with increasing internet penetration in India, e-commerce has become a significant sales channel for the brand. Dilip says, 'Because of e-commerce, Hidesign has been able to reach to places where it would have never reached otherwise. But by giving high discounts, e-commerce channels reduce the aspirational value of the brand.' Along with its advantages, e-commerce has some drawbacks. The kind of storytelling and experience that is provided at offline stores can't be provided online. Though the brand stories are communicated through brand pages on websites like Amazon and Flipkart, customers don't necessarily visit brand pages. If they are looking for a product, most of the time, they go directly to the category page. So, they miss out on brand communication.

In mass markets, brands distribute their products across organised and unorganised channels because they want to reach and please the broadest possible spectrum of customers. Luxury brands, in contrast, are focused on creating a very focused experience for the right customers. The company does not distribute to the unorganised sector as it cannot control the service, the display and the quality of ambiance.

Hidesign is expanding its market by capturing exclusive and strategic retail spaces across all major metros and airports in India. It is also targeting tier-2 and tier-3 cities that display a growing consumer profile. As of December 2019, Hidesign had around 100 exclusive boutiques in India. Over the next three to five years, Dilip wanted to see Hidesign as a more established brand in tier-2, and some tier-3 cities in India, with over 200 stores and 300–400 store-in-stores. He expected a steady growth of 20–30 per cent every year and wanted to establish the brand in other Asian countries as well.

Create a business in harmony with the environment

Larry Ellison said, 'If you do everything that everyone else does in business, you're going to lose. The only way to really be ahead is to "be different".' The leather industry is considered one of the most polluting industries. While many leather brands do not pay attention to the environmental effects caused by leather production, Hidesign has been different and has made numerous efforts to protect and preserve the natural environment.

While most of the industry players have been focusing on the cheaper and faster chemical tanning process, Hidesign has been a leader in the research and use of vegetable tanned leathers for its leather goods. The vegetable tanning process is environment-friendly, but it is 30 per cent more expensive and takes more than double the time to produce as compared to chemical tanning. But it gives a deep leather colour, good body and long-lasting strength. On the other hand, the chemical tanning process is carcinogenic and a significant polluter of the environment.

When people think about leather factories, images of unclean working environments appear in their minds; especially those who have seen cities like Kanpur in Uttar Pradesh know the ways in which the leather industry has devastated the ecosystem. Heavy metal compounds used in tanning have even polluted the river Ganga (the lifeline of North India), but Hidesign is very different. Its factory was designed by the acclaimed ceramic artist Ray Meeker. The factory campus is green. It uses no asbestos, only bricks, and is surrounded by ponds, streams and waterfalls that recharge groundwater and aid in natural filtration. The workshop is constructed from bricks made of local earth and fired in kilns that were made on the premises. The premises where artisans work reflect brand values. Lunch time is pretty much outdoors, under the trees, sitting on rock benches and tables. At Hidesign, no workspace holds more than 100 people at a given time with ample organised workspace for every artisan.

Ecology and sustainability are core values of Hidesign. All waste water from the tannery is filtered using RO (reverse osmosis) and reused. All waste material is separated and reused or sold for reuse and the brand even gave up plastic packaging. Solar panels take care of electricity consumption. Furthermore, nothing is burnt at the factory.

Along with minimising waste, Hidesign also ran an environmental project—The Green Story—in collaboration with Joss Brooks. Brooks grew up in the Australian state of Tasmania, a place full of wild natural beauty, and came to

Auroville in 1970, after having lived in Europe and Africa. He joined the early pioneering efforts in land restoration at Auroville and founded the Pitchandikulam community in 1973, which is now a vibrant 60-acre forest with 800 species of plants in the grasslands, a nursery and an ethnomedicinal forest. Joss's love of nature has been a constant source of inspiration to Hidesign. The company works with Joss and his team at Pitchandikulam forest to support this conservation work.

Together, they are working on three beneficial fields of conservation: afforestation, medicinal plants and wildlife. The afforestation project aims to cover land around Puducherry, planting approximately 7,000 indigenous trees that will foster an ecosystem for insects and other animals native to the forests. In the Kaliveli bioregion in South India, where Hidesign is supporting Joss Brooks's work, more than 400 species of medicinal plants are being used by the local people for the preparation of remedies and medicines.

In 2016, with Joss Brooks, Hidesign launched a new environmental campaign called 'The Green Story – It Starts with a Seed'. Hidesign has been actively promoting this project with the launch of a special range of packaging—cloth and paper bags that have beautiful illustrations of plants and animals. Hidesign's annual diary celebrates animals and nature. Moreover, Hidesign has collaborated with Sri Aurobindo Ashram's handmade paper unit in Puducherry, which produced over 10,000 paper tags with seeds embedded in them. These paper tags are freely distributed amongst all customers, encouraging them to start their own garden.

Having grown up in Puducherry, Dilip has lived very closely with nature. So, anything that disturbs nature's balance is unpardonable to him. Creative satisfaction and responsibility towards the environment continue to remain driving forces for him, rather than selling more bags and expanding his brand reach. He says, 'I want our brand to be relevant and one that improves the lives of those who use it and makes them happy. We want to stay natural and ecological. That is very important to us.'

Surprise and delight your customers

Dilip says, 'The core of a brand is to create desire.' Desire to own a brand comes from the value the brand adds to the life of the customer. A brand usually offers two types of value: functional and symbolic.

Functional value emerges from the features and the potential uses of the product. As a brand, Hidesign never follows trends. Dilip believes that with trends, you follow what other big brands have done, and become a copycat. Following trends is a great model for mass-market labels and lacks creativity. Instead of following trends, the Hidesign team follows lifestyle changes. In a country like India, changes are so rapid that five years is a generation. You need to listen to your customers, observe changes in their lifestyle, and follow them. From the perspective of functional value, Hidesign's team focuses on every minute aspect of their customers' lifestyles, such as how they live, how they function, what could help them, what could irritate them, how they dress, what they carry, what they have stopped carrying—the list goes on. They understand that a Hidesign bag is an investment and ensure that it remains current for at least a few years. They bring out 50–60 new styles every season, which is phenomenal in contemporary terms. Dilip says, 'The brand has essentially not changed since it started. Its core values are still the same—natural, ecological and innovative. The changes that take place only reflect the changing lifestyle of the customer base.'

Symbolic value emerges from the social standing of a brand, that is, the extent to which the brand is perceived as being an elite offering aspired by customers. It helps elevate the customer in terms of prestige, status and value. One way to emphasise the brand's symbolic value is by communicating its longstanding heritage. Hidesign, while international in its outlook, is very much rooted in its own heritage of Puducherry, with its commitment to handcrafting and its love for nature. Hidesign's stores communicate stories of craftsmanship and transport customers to its much-loved hometown, Puducherry.

From the perspective of symbolic value, physical environments have always been central to luxury brands. They curate the customer experience with exclusive locations, exceptional service and beautifully designed interiors. As is common in all Hidesign stores, the fixtures of the store are handmade with natural materials such as wood, solid brass and natural grain leather, creating a fresh and unusual look that the brand is recognised for. The personalised service provided at all the stores informs the customer of the exclusive nature of Hidesign, advises the customers of what is best suited to their needs, and in case of a problem, promptly solves it. The company is very selective in its hiring process and trains the store staff to connect and communicate with its customers.

The Hidesign flagship store in Puducherry is one of India's largest concept stores set up by a luxury brand. This store is spread over four sprawling levels. The first level has clean, sparse displays for Hidesign's latest collections. The second level showcases Hidesign's men's bags and a collage of its ad campaigns. The third level showcases the brand's history through its timeline and travel section. This store also has some of the most significant milestones from Hidesign's past, including its iconic products. The antique furniture in the store is complemented by magnificent blue cut-glass chandeliers, which create a refreshing visual experience. Hidesign builds on its vision of a global luxury brand by presenting contemporary installations throughout the store, created by artists from around the world who have settled in Puducherry. On the pillars across the store are pictures of the 'People of Hidesign', that is, individuals who have helped build the brand, and the 'Stores of Hidesign' across the world, which bring a remarkable charm to the store. Recently, the store has been redesigned by Ayaz Basrai and Dilip, paying homage to the architecture of Puducherry with an entire section on sustainability.

Another interesting example is Hidesign's store at the Hyderabad airport that offers the option of customisation and personalisation. Customers can choose to personalise their bag with their name or initials on it for free, or design their bag from scratch and get it delivered for free anywhere across the world. They can even pick the shape, colour, buckles and lining to create their ideal bag exclusively made for them, an experience everyone with a taste for luxury loves. Similarly, other exclusive stores also exude an atmosphere that reflects an environment of luxury and custom-made products.

Luxury carries its heritage, place of origin, story and sense of time to connect with its audience. When Dilip first met Yves Carcelle, then President of Louis Vuitton, he received a piece of valuable advice: 'Great brands take decades to build, the journey and story of every brand is unique and precious.' Inspired by that advice, Dilip decided to endorse Hidesign's heritage and document its story through the *Icon Book*. Bound in Hidesign's vegetable tanned goat leather, the *Icon Book* reflects the rich history and rebellious character of Hidesign and its founder Dilip Kapur's journey over the years. In 2014, the company relaunched 11 of its most beloved bags, and called them 'The Icons'. These bags with their whimsical designs were individualistic and full of character. They stood for what the company loved best—a spirit of adventure, clean designs and the use of natural materials. A special exhibition of museum bags, banned advertisements and archival photographs was curated by Dilip and presented for display at premium malls in Delhi, Mumbai and Bengaluru, along with the *Icon Book*. Symbolically, this exhibition began at the Aurobindo Ashram in Puducherry.

Dilip says, 'As you expand, there is always a danger of losing who you are. We needed to go back and relook at who we were. We needed to go back to our roots so that we continue with the same values. That was one of the main reasons we wanted to do the *Icon Book* and the Icon Exhibition. When Louis Vuitton invested in us, they told us not to make the mistake that most of the Indian companies have made: pretending to be European. They told us to tell the world who we are.'

Dilip's own vision, lifestyle, authenticity and emotional quotient have played a significant role in building Hidesign as one of the world's most desirable brands. He has never formally studied design but has always designed his bags. Despite receiving no formal leather training, he has created a leather brand that has an incredible aura of its own. And without having any business degree, he has created a highly successful business. It is his love for the art of design and leather crafts that has helped him achieve what people are not able to with degrees and all kinds of other support.

As a grateful entrepreneur, Dilip continuously thanks his alma mater for shaping his mind and his brand. He says, 'In the Sri Aurobindo Ashram, I was part of the free system of education. The school at the Ashram gave me the freedom and the ability to think independently. Phillips Academy, one of the toughest schools in the United States, taught me discipline and ambition. Princeton taught me to think and solve problems, while the cultural revolution in the late 1960s at Princeton greatly influenced my rebellion against uniformity and a plastic culture.' He also remains grateful to numerous people from the Auroville community who helped shape his journey. The modest advice from The Mother at Sri Aurobindo Ashram, that influenced Dilip all through his childhood—'There is great beauty in simplicity'—is still the underlying design philosophy that drives Hidesign.

Dilip starts his day early with yoga and a set of simple exercises followed by meditation. His interests, like reading, swimming at the beach, long walks in the forest with his dogs, etc., act as excellent sources of ideas for him. For instance, once, Dilip visited Kenya for the launch of Hidesign there. Over the weekend, he flew to Maasai Mara, one of Africa's greatest wildlife reserves.

He was inspired by the synergy of the Maasai people with nature, their heritage of crafting beads, spears and hides. He thought about creating a collection that would be modern yet reflect the elegance and grace of the Maasai people. It took him and his team about six months to design the range and another two months to craft it. His team had a lot of fun experimenting with brass, creating masks, spears and shields that were then used as a part of the bag fittings. This fascination resulted in a whole new range of Hidesign bags called The Maasai Collection. Similarly, Hidesign has come up with many other collections in collaboration with Disney, the Italian designer Alberto Ciaschini, the French designer Jose Levy, the Bollywood actor Kalki Koechlin and others.

Once a brand is known for a set of standards, it is always crucial to meet them. Consistency is key to ensuring your customers become and remain loyal. Today, around 70 per cent of the visitors to Hidesign stores are people who already own a Hidesign product.

Dilip's journey of creating one of the most respected global brands from his hobby is truly remarkable. But beyond creating an iconic brand, Dilip has made a positive difference in the lives of many. The Indian caste system has placed cobblers at the bottom, among untouchables and outcastes. They were traditionally at the mercy of higher caste landlords. But by valuing the cobblers' inherited understanding and love of leather, Hidesign has offered them a platform through which to display their handiwork and gain admiration and respect for it. Those who work at Hidesign feel free from social imprisonment and encourage their children to educate themselves and rise above the hierarchy. Hidesign has also empowered women from the cobbler caste by creating jobs for them, so they are no longer at the mercy of men who drink and abuse them. Today, the brand's workforce of 3,000 people has 90 per cent female members.

Moving forward, Hidesign is expanding its footprint both in Indian and international markets. It would be interesting to see how this brand evolves in its next phase of growth.

DILIP KAPUR

Advice from Dilip Kapur

- Don't follow trends. If you follow trends like everyone else, then you can't be different. Differentiate yourself.
- You need to communicate and advertise where your customers are. If customers move, you should also move.
- If you try to fight a price war, you can't win as there will always be someone cheaper than you. You have to create desire.
- When you become too risk-averse, you become too boring. Make your mistakes, but don't be boring.
- Mistakes happen when you ignore things and leave them to others. It is important for a leader to do reviews. This process may sound boring, but it should be done systematically. Amazing things can happen when reviews are done, and terrible things can happen when reviews are not done.

SUPER30

Creating avenues for growth at the bottom of the pyramid

Though Bihar is considered to be one of the poorest states in India, it has a very rich history. It is the birthplace of the Maurya Empire, which was one of the largest empires in the world. It is the place where Prince Siddhartha Gautama became the Buddha and laid the foundation of Buddhism, one of the most widely practised religions in the world. It is the place where Nalanda University, one of the first universities in the world, was established. In fact, Aryabhata, the father of Indian mathematics, was born in Bihar. The list of jewels in the crown of Bihar goes on. This is the story of one such jewel—Super 30.

Founded in 2002, Super 30 is a non-profit programme that provides free coaching along with food and accommodation to 30 poor students selected through a written test every year. These students are nurtured to crack IIT-JEE, a highly competitive entrance exam for the Indian Institutes of Technology (IITs), the most prestigious engineering institutes in India. The person behind this programme is a mathematician—Anand Kumar.

It was Anand's dream to study at the University of Cambridge in England, one of the world's top universities for mathematics and the alma mater of influential scientists like Sir Isaac Newton. Although Anand got admission there, he was not able to study at Cambridge because of his poor financial condition and the sudden death of his father. His dream remained a dream. But he decided to help other people, those from poor backgrounds, turn their dreams into reality. Because of his programme Super 30, the children of rickshaw-pullers, farm labourers, autorickshaw drivers, housemaids and others have been able to study at premier institutes in India. The success rate of Super 30 has been phenomenal. By 2019, 440 out of 510 students had made it to the IITs. The remaining had qualified for the National Institutes of Technology (NITs) and other top engineering colleges.

Because of its impact, Super 30 has been recognised by many national and international organisations. For instance, *Time* magazine included Super 30 in its list of The Best of Asia in 2010, *Newsweek* magazine included it in its list of the four most innovative schools in the world, former US President Barack Obama's special envoy Rashad Hussain termed it the best institute in the country, among other accolades.

Anand's efforts in the field of education are considered pioneering. He has received numerous awards, including the Maulana Abul Kalam Azad Shiksha Puraskar, the highest honour given by the state government of Bihar in the field of education. He has also received Rashtriya Bal Kalyan Award by the former President of India Shri Ram Nath Kovind. He has delivered lectures at famed institutions like MIT, Harvard, Stanford, Cambridge, Tokyo University, University of British Columbia, IITs and IIMs, and has been featured by media across the globe, including *The New York Times*, Monocle, Discovery Channel, BBC, Japanese and French TV channels, Japan's NHK, among others. Moreover, the Bollywood movie *Super 30* starring Hrithik Roshan is based on Anand's life.

This chapter covers the inspiring journey of Super 30, one of the most impactful brands in India.

THE BEGINNING

Anand was born in Gaudiya Math, a slum in the small town of Mithapur, a suburb of Patna. His father, Rajendra Prasad, worked as a clerk in the railway mail service. Since childhood, he was quite a mischievous and curious boy. He wanted to know the why and the how behind everything. While other kids were content with playing with their toys, Anand's joy came from opening up toys to see how they worked. As he grew up, his family members and neighbours became used to Anand's tendency to solve challenges.

His father always said to him, 'I have high hopes for you. If you really want to become a scientist, you will have to study well. Mathematics is the key, as it is required in science also.' Anand developed an interest in mathematics while studying at a Hindi-medium government school.

The mathematician who inspired Anand the most was Srinivasa Ramanujan. Born in 1887, Ramanujan was a self-taught mathematician working as a clerk in a post office in India. Working alone, he discovered unknown mathematical results that were far ahead of his time. In 1913, he sent a letter filled with mathematical theorems to G.H. Hardy, a mathematician at the University of Cambridge. Recognising Ramanujan's work as extraordinary, Hardy arranged for him to travel to Cambridge. Ramanujan spent nearly five years in Cambridge collaborating with Hardy. During his short life span of 32 years, Ramanujan left behind around 4,000 original mathematical ideas and formulas.

In 1993, Anand's paper was published in *Mathematical Spectrum*, a prestigious British journal. This publication increased his confidence, and he went on to publish a few more papers in prestigious journals, including *The Mathematical Gazette*. With time, Anand started getting recognised as an emerging mathematician. Based on his work published in journals, Anand got admission into the University of Cambridge.

Everything had been finalised, and he was supposed to join the university on 1 October 1994. His father made many unsuccessful efforts to arrange the money for his studies. But, as fate would have it, his father suddenly passed away almost a month-and-a-half before he was scheduled to leave. It was a tough time, but Anand's friends and family pressed him to continue the search for the funds for Cambridge. He did not even have the money to buy an airplane ticket at the time. Unfortunately, no voluntary organisation, no businessman, no minister came forward when he needed help. Time passed, and Anand missed the opportunity to fulfil his dream.

After his father's death, Anand was offered a clerical job on the grounds of compassion, but he was not keen on taking it up. He wanted to pursue his dreams in the field of mathematics. Thankfully, his family was supportive, despite all their hardships. His mother, Jayanti Devi, encouraged him to chase his dreams. She used to make papads and Anand would sell the papads during the day and study at night. Meanwhile, he started tutoring a few students at the Ramanujan School of Mathematics, an institution Anand named in honour of the great mathematician who was his role model.

One day, a boy named Abhishek Kumar came to see Anand. He was barefoot and wearing a tattered t-shirt. He shared his aspiration to become an engineer with Anand, but he had no money to pay the tuition fee. Anand was a bit sceptical, so in the evening, he went to see Abhishek at the given address and found him studying by the light of a street lamp. Ever since his Cambridge dream had been shattered, Anand had empathised with students who encountered such monetary obstacles. He knew that Bihar was a repository of talented youngsters, but a large number of them did not get the right platform to hone their talent because of financial constraints. Many of them had to forego higher education, as their families did not have adequate resources to support them. He asked himself, why was he not thinking about them.

While coming back home, he recalled his father's words about having a higher purpose in life. He decided that he would do something to help those who couldn't afford proper education.

THE BRAND NAME: SUPER 30

Small incidents give rise to big achievements, especially when triggered by agony. Anand decided to select 30 bright students from poor families and prepare them for IIT-JEE, free of cost. He had arrived at the number 30 after much thought; taking on 50 students would be beyond his means. To separate these students from the dismal conditions of their everyday lives and create an environment to study, Anand wanted to fund their stay and food.

As arranging food from outside would have been expensive, he asked his mother if she could cook food for 30 students every day. He told his mother, 'By educating these children, I can help them elevate their entire family and village.' His mother looked at Anand with pride but was not sure how Anand would achieve his dream. She said, 'You think yourself to be a Superman!' Anand's brother Pranav was listening to this conversation and interrupted them by saying, 'Bhaiya, maybe you should name these students Super 30.' He had created this name by combining 30 (the number of students) with the word 'Super', which had clicked when his mother said 'Superman'. Seeing her sons' determination, Jayanti Devi agreed to support this initiative. Anand took her blessings and started Super 30 in 2002. Pranav came forward to take care of the administrative part of the programme so that Anand could focus on preparing the coursework.

BUSINESS LESSONS

Many important business lessons can be learnt from the evolution of this phenomenal brand—Super 30. A few of them are as follows.

Continuously reinvent yourself

George Bernard Shaw said, 'Life isn't about finding yourself. Life is about creating yourself.' Since his childhood, Anand has made a lot of effort in creating his journey to becoming a mathematician. By the time he reached Class X, Anand had started showing signs of becoming a mathematical genius. His teachers would also talk about his aptitude for the subject. Upon completing Class X, he secured admission to B.N. College in Patna. There, he started exploring new things in mathematics that he learnt from journals and solving complex questions from various other sources. He realised that the kind of mathematics he had studied till Class X was mostly theoretical, and he needed to go deeper into the subject. He started approaching Professor Devi Prasad Verma, the head of the mathematics department at Patna Science College, Professor Balgangadhar Prasad of B.N. College, and Professor Mohammed Shahabuddin of the Bihar College of Engineering (now NIT Patna) on a regular basis to ask questions and clear doubts. His persistence while solving problems impressed his teachers.

Anand was aware of his ability to explain mathematics to others, and he used to help his fellow students at Patna University in solving their doubts. In 1992, he began a little mathematics club with two students. The club was dedicated to discussion about the subject and used to run for two to three hours a day, three to five days a week. Word soon got around and teachers and students started coming to the club to discuss mathematics with Anand. To make the subject interesting, Anand drew connections between mathematics and real life. By 1993, Anand's club had become popular, and nearly 40 students had enrolled in it to study for a nominal fee of ₹25 every month, which was almost one-tenth of the fees coaching classes were charging in those days. Most of this amount was spent on rent for the teaching room and to make arrangements for drinking water. As Anand had some income now, he started considering enrolling for higher education.

He would read books on mathematics written by American and Russian authors, that were made available to him by vendors selling second-hand books. Anand would even read biographies of famous mathematicians. The University of Cambridge often featured in these biographies, as a place that had helped many geniuses hone their mathematical talent. He started dreaming of attending this great institution. Meanwhile, Anand's brother Pranav, who was passionate about music, began to learn the violin under the guidance of Dr N. Rajam of the Banaras Hindu University (BHU) in Varanasi. This allowed Anand to visit BHU and explore its library, which was a treasure trove of mathematics journals. Since the library at Patna University did not have foreign journals, Anand would travel to Varanasi (where his brother had a hostel room) every weekend, undertaking a six-hour long train journey. There, he would spend Saturday and Sunday at the Central Library, BHU, and return to Patna on Monday morning. He would sit in the library for hours to solve challenging problems until the librarian switched off the lights to get rid of him.

Once, he solved a complicated mathematical problem, which had remained unsolved till then, and shared it with Professor Devi Prasad Verma. Professor Verma helped him present his solution better in the form of a publishable research paper. Anand knew Kaushal Ajitabh, who was seven or eight years older than him and who was pursuing his PhD at MIT in the USA. Anand requested him to review his paper. Kaushal was very impressed by Anand's work and helped him edit the paper. Both Professor Verma and Kaushal encouraged Anand to send his paper for publication.

After a lot of hard work Anand's paper titled 'Happy Numbers' was published in *Mathematical Spectrum*, a prestigious British journal. He went on to publish a few more papers, including one in the century-old prestigious journal—*The Mathematical Gazette*. In April 1994, he filled up an application form for the University of Cambridge, attached his published papers, and sent the envelope without the application fee, as he didn't have the means to pay it. A month later, a letter arrived at Anand's house while he was getting ready for college. He opened the letter and found that his application had been accepted by the university. Everything had been finalised, and he was supposed to enrol there on 1 October 1994. But as fate would have it, his father suddenly passed away almost a month and a half before he was scheduled to leave. He didn't have the money and had to support his family as its primary earner. Sadly, he missed his dream opportunity!

Steve Jobs once said, 'Sometimes life is going to hit you in the head with a brick. Don't lose faith.' From the pain of losing the opportunity to go to Cambridge emerged the inspiration to set up Super 30. Anand established Super 30 to nurture and groom talented students, from the poorest of families, for admission to the IITs. The success rate of the Super 30 programme has been close to 90 per cent, and it has become a globally recognised institute.

Rather than resting on these laurels, Anand continuously tries to upgrade himself in order to benefit his students. He says, 'As a teacher, I have to reinvent myself constantly. I can't hand out the same notes that I used 15 years ago to my current students.' To keep abreast of trends in pedagogy, Anand attends workshops and sessions, such as the ones hosted by the Mathematical Association of America. He also listens to experts and reads the latest books and journals.

Anand's story is an inspiring example of how perseverance, courage and a positive attitude to life can help people transform their failure into a ladder to the top. And how even after reaching the top, such people reinvent themselves continuously.

Don't crib about today, create a new tomorrow

Whenever we talk about the impact of a teacher on a student, the examples of Chanakya and Chandragupta come to mind. Chanakya was a vastly learned Brahmin from Takshashila. He had come to Pataliputra (now Patna), for higher recognition. But the ruling king of Magadha, Dhana Nanda, offended and insulted him. Chandragupta was a boy living in Pataliputra in poverty and was employed by a hunter to look after his cattle. One day, Chanakya saw Chandragupta while he was playing the role of king amongst his playmates and giving judgment. Chanakya was impressed by his intelligence as well as his individuality. He took the boy with him from Pataliputra to Takshashila to educate him for a significant role in the future.

Chandragupta emerged as an able military commander and a great leader, who ended Dhana Nanda's empire. Under the guidance of Chanakya, Chandragupta founded the Maurya Empire, which became one of the largest empires the world has ever seen. Chanakya made the world realise that someone who is fit to rule should be king, irrespective of whether or not they are the king's son.

Being a man with limited means, Anand's father had big dreams for his son. He often said to Anand, 'I don't know why, but I feel you will do something big.' Taking inspiration from his father's words, Anand always tried to create a better tomorrow not only for himself but also for his students. In the way that Chanakya picked up Chandragupta and turned him into a righteous king, every year Anand picks 30 students and turns them into role models.

There are many inspiring stories of poor students who managed to transform their lives after studying at Super 30, creating a better tomorrow for themselves, their families and their villages. One compelling story is that of Shivangi, who sold newspapers and magazines with her father. Despite the hardships she faced, Shivangi did not give up on her academics. She would study at every given opportunity, and she finished her intermediate education from a government school in Deha, a small place in Uttar Pradesh, situated 60 km from Kanpur. One day Shivangi read about Super 30 and decided to visit Anand. Soon she became a part of the programme. Shivangi joined the Chemical Engineering programme at IIT Roorkee. When she was facing problems with paying the fee, Super 30 helped her get an education loan from a bank by giving the required guarantee. Today, Shivangi works with a reputed firm.

Nidhi Jha is another Super 30 alumni. Her father is a Class VI dropout and drives a rented auto-rickshaw in the lanes of Varanasi. Her father was upset when she was born as the third daughter of a poor family. She had tried to crack the IIT entrance in Class XII but did not succeed. One day, she read about Super 30 in a newspaper. She appeared for the Super 30 entrance and got selected. Because there are fewer girls in the programme, Nidhi stayed with Anand's family while the boys resided in a rented hostel nearby. From Super 30, she went to study at the prestigious Indian School of Mines (now IIT Dhanbad) and then went on to work with L&T in Delhi. Pascal Pinson, a French director, has included Nidhi's journey in his documentary *The Big Day*. Nidhi's parents, Anand and Pranav attended the film's premiere in Paris along with her and were proud to see Nidhi's posters on the streets of the city.

Abhishek Raj was born in a remote village in Bihar in a poor farming family, his mother often had to go out to labour to supplement the household income. He joined Super 30 and went on to study Geophysics at IIT Kharagpur before moving to Houston, USA, and then to England, for work.

One more student, Shashi Narayan, the son of a worker in a government hospital, won the Erasmus Mundus scholarship for research in France and went on to take up a teaching position in England.

There are many such stories of Super 30 students that make us realise that situations can be tough, if people work hard, they can create a better tomorrow.

Today, Super 30 doesn't need an introduction. Because of the success of its students, it has become a household name. Although these students and their parents remember Anand for the difference he has made in their lives, Anand says, 'These students don't have the advantage of English-medium education and unlimited resources, but they work really hard—often for 14 to 16 hours a day, seven days a week. And that's the secret behind their success in the IIT-JEE.'

Great input generates great output

IIT-JEE is considered one of the toughest exams in the world. Every year, lakhs of students apply for this exam, and only 1 per cent of them succeed. The demand for coaching institutes for IIT-JEE is so high that the coaching industry is valued at billions of rupees. Children who come from well-to-do families have the luxury of studying in plush schools and top-notch coaching institutes. But the children who come from poor families and rural areas manage to attend only ill-equipped government schools that are devoid of basic amenities like laboratories, libraries and qualified teachers. Very few teachers take the pains to understand the restlessness of the poor students, whose curiosity remains unsatisfied. Yet, the students manage to clear their primary and secondary education from these schools. For them, there are no options, and they have to accept whatever is available to them in the name of education.

To show significant results, every coaching institute looks for great students. At the same time, to achieve their dreams, every good student searches for a great teacher. In the first batch of Super 30, 18 students cleared IIT-JEE. Though the results of the first batch of Super 30 would have encouraged meritorious students to apply for the programme in the subsequent years, you might still wonder why students from remote areas decide to study with Anand in Patna. Before starting Super 30, for a few years, Anand ran many short (10–15 days) training camps, workshops and crash courses in Patna. To create awareness about these programmes, Anand's brother Pranav used to distribute pamphlets in the city and nearby villages. Students would attend these courses, as they understood that education was a channel through which they could rise above poverty.

As there was no fee to be paid for the programme, and students wanted to learn unique methods to solve complex problems, they began coming to attend Anand's classes. Due to a lack of funds, Anand didn't have a proper place to hold these workshops, so Pranav would sit for hours near a landmark to direct students to where the class was being held. As students started liking what they were learning, word of mouth started spreading. By 2002, Anand had become a known name in villages around Patna. Though there was no defined fee for these programmes, students started paying some money (5, 10, 25 rupees) voluntarily, because they liked what they got, while there were students who despite liking Anand's classes could not pay him anything.

In 2002, Anand announced an entrance exam for his newly created programme Super 30, which would provide free education, food and stay to 30 students and would prepare them for IIT entrance. To spread awareness about this programme, Pranav travelled on his cycle across Patna and the nearby villages and distributed pamphlets. A few local newspapers also covered the announcement of this free coaching programme. Word of mouth spread, and thousands of students appeared for the entrance test. Anand selected the 30 students and started his first batch. In 2005, Anand created a website for Super 30 that helped in spreading word about the programme. Now, every year, the Ramanujan School of Mathematics holds a competitive test. About 800 to 1,000 students appear for the test, and eventually, the programme selects 30 bright students from underprivileged families.

Anand's mother, Jayanti Devi, cooks for the students, and his brother Pranav Kumar takes care of the management. Anand teaches with the help of a small faculty consisting of four more teachers, all equally dedicated to go to any length to uphold his cause of helping the underprivileged. Anand has never taken any donations from anyone. To support the programme and his family's expenses, in the evenings, Anand holds three-hour classes at the Ramanujan School of Mathematics, for students who come from families that can pay the fee. His wife, Ritu, an alumnus of IIT Varanasi, also supports Anand by setting test papers for the students.

Dr A.P.J. Abdul Kalam said, 'If you want to shine like a sun, first burn like a sun.' Students who get into Super 30 commit themselves to a 16-hours-a-day-7-days-a-week study routine for a year.

Anand not only works on their education but also puts in a lot of effort in increasing their self-confidence. Even in the hostel, students help each other with their studies and maintain an environment of healthy competition. Anand says, 'I do not claim to have a success formula. I essentially teach them to be innovative, work hard, and develop patience and a positive outlook. Most importantly, I instil in them a thirst for knowledge.'

After the success of Super 30 and its growing popularity, Anand received offers of financial assistance from business leaders like Mukesh Ambani and Anand Mahindra as well as the government, but he has refused them all. He lives a simple life, eats simple food and takes his classes in a lower-middle-class colony amidst factories, buffalo sheds and crumbling huts.

Patience and focus are the keys to building a successful brand

N.R. Narayana Murthy said, 'Performance leads to recognition. Recognition brings respect. Respect enhances power. Humility and grace in one's moments of power enhance the dignity of an organisation.' Today, Super 30 is one of the most respected education brands in the world, and Anand Kumar is India's most famous teacher for IIT entrance preparation. But, behind the current recognition of Super 30, there are years of hard work.

Anand has been a columnist for various national and international mathematical journals and magazines. In fact, for many years, he taught for free or for a nominal fee. His ability to simplify the complexities of mathematics made him popular among students. In 2003, 18 students from Super 30 were selected at IITs. Many people thought this was because of a one-time luck factor. But then, in 2004, the number of Super 30 students who cleared the IIT-JEE rose to 22. As luck would have it, *The New York Times* covered the journeys of a few poor students from India, who made it to the prestigious IITs. These students gave credit for their success to Super 30, and this was, in a way, the first recognition earned by Super 30.

Around the same time, the Japanese channel NHK noticed Super 30 and made the first documentary on the programme. In 2005, the number of Super 30 students who cleared the IIT entrance exam rose from 22 to 26. Then, *The Guardian* covered Super 30. This was followed by a visit from Japanese actress and former Miss Japan Norika Fujiwara to shoot another documentary on Super 30 in 2007. Japan has lauded the programme in many ways. Over the years, Super 30 has been part of several Japanese documentaries and books, and some of the Super 30 students have even received scholarships for higher studies in Japan.

Inspiringly, in 2008, all the 30 students from Super 30 cracked the IIT-JEE. In 2009, again, all the 30 students cracked the IIT entrance exam. This was the time when Discovery Channel made a documentary on Super 30, and Anand was also featured by the BBC. In 2009, he was also inducted in the *Limca Book of Records* for his contribution to helping poor students. In 2010, again, all 30 students from the Super 30 cracked the IIT entrance exam. This time, former US President Barack Obama's special envoy, Rashad Hussain, visited Super 30 and called it the best institute in the country. After this, recognition and encouragement started flowing. In 2010, *Time* magazine named Super 30 as the best school in Asia. Then, *Newsweek* listed Super 30 as one of the four most innovative schools in the world. In 2010, Anand was awarded Maulana Abdul Kalam Azad Shiksha Puraskar, the top award of the Bihar government.

In 2011, Anand was selected by the European magazine *FOCUS* as one of the global personalities who have the ability to shape exceptionally talented people. Around the same time, Anand also helped Amitabh Bachchan prepare for his role in the Bollywood film *Aarakshan*, in which Amitabh Bachchan played the role of a teacher, who teaches mathematics to underprivileged students. In 2012, Anand was included in the list of 20 pioneering teachers of the world by UK-based magazine *Monocle*. He was also honoured by the government of British Columbia, Canada. In 2014, Anand was honoured with the prestigious Ramanujan Mathematics Award at the Eighth National Mathematics Convention. Anand has received many other national and international recognitions, including the Rashtriya Bal Kalyan Award by the then President of India Ram Nath Kovind. In 2019, the Bollywood movie *Super 30* starring Hrithik Roshan made Anand and Super 30 household names.

Over the years, Anand has spoken about his life and his work at various global-level institutes, including Harvard, MIT, Stanford, IIM Ahmedabad, several IITs, University of British Columbia, Tokyo University and many others. In 2019, he was invited to deliver a lecture at the University of Cambridge, the university of his erstwhile dreams, that he hadn't been able to attend due to financial constraints.

To cash in on Super 30's brand value, many fake Super 30s have mushroomed prefixed with names such as Gaya, Nalanda, Raja, Baja, among many others. These institutes take donations from governments and private institutions and even take high fees from students. Anand has made numerous efforts to communicate that he doesn't take any donations, and Super 30 doesn't have any other branches. The rise of Super 30 has also given a blow to the education mafia and the money-making coaching industry. Anand and his team have received numerous death threats and have been attacked multiple times.

Anand goes through tremendous hardships in sustaining his academy. But avoiding the fame he has received, he is focused on making an impact through education. He says, 'In the end, the difference between the privileged and underprivileged is only of opportunity. If all get equal opportunity to quality education, India will move ahead faster.'

Storytelling is the most powerful way to bring change

Annette Simmons said, 'If you wish to influence an individual or a group to embrace a particular value in their daily lives, tell them a compelling story.' As Super 30 students belong to extremely poor backgrounds, Anand understands that along with teaching, he has to instill confidence in them. Anand says, 'More than the physical distance, there's the psychological and social distance between poor students and the IITs.' Interestingly, he uses stories to create an atmosphere for the optimal growth of each one of them.

To motivate his students, Anand has created two cartoon characters—Ricky and Bholu. He uses these characters while teaching his classes. Ricky is a rich, urban boy with an English-medium background. He eats pizzas, burgers and hot dogs, and wears designer clothes. Bholu, on the other hand, is a poor boy who eats dal, roti and vegetables. He wears ordinary clothes, ordinary slippers and speaks rural dialects. In his classroom, Anand shows how Ricky struggles to solve one question in a single way, while Bholu easily solves the same question in ten different ways. It is Bholu who invariably turns out to be the winner. Students instantly relate to the cartoon characters that relax them and open them up.

Anand's stories have a significant impact on his students. For instance, one of the Super 30 students, Anup, came from a Maoist-prone rural Aurangabad school, which had not given him a strong base in science and mathematics. Since Hindi had been the medium of instruction for him so far, he was also awfully short on confidence. Years ago, his father had gone out to bring food, and had not returned since. His mother barely earned ₹100 a day by doing odd, menial jobs. After he passed Class XII, she took him to Chief Minister Nitish Kumar's Janata Darbar in Patna, where somebody told her about Super 30.

In the IIT-JEE, Anup finished his paper ten minutes before the scheduled time while others were still struggling. Surprised, someone asked him: 'What is your name?' Anup replied: 'Bholu.' He cried inconsolably after making it to IIT Bombay. Today, Anup is a successful serial entrepreneur. He co-founded a health startup, a gaming solutions company, and is currently the founder of a coaching platform. Anand says, 'I had created these cartoon characters to make my students believe in their abilities.'

Anand shares that when Suresh, the son of a daily wage worker at a brick-kiln and one of the successful candidates from the 2005 batch of Super 30, was studying at IIT Delhi, some foreigners who were doing a survey asked him if he had any inferiority complex. Suresh shot back, 'Why should I feel any complex when I am the topper in my class?' Anand said that another Super 30 student, Shashi Narayan, the son of a compounder, had got a low rank in the 2004 IIT-JEE. He subsequently got the architectural engineering programme at IIT Kharagpur. But in the first year itself, he worked so hard that he managed to get computer science for his second year, creating a kind of record there. Now, Shashi is a senior scientist in the Google office in London.

Anand says, 'Making students memorise defeats the purpose.' In his classes, he explains the rationale behind concepts and formulas. He also encourages students to think about what new things they can do, what innovations they can come up with, and how many ways they can solve a problem. For example, different methods are taught to calculate the area of a triangle, thereby providing varied perspectives to one problem. Similarly, the rationale behind mathematical equations like $(a+b)^2$ is explained to help students appreciate the logic. These methods go a long way in creating a student's life-long interest in mathematics and making the subject engaging and creative.

Anand not only teaches students how to crack the exam but also how to conquer different problems in life. He continually shares stories of the struggles and the successes of previous students to inspire new students. He says, 'The moment a student joins my institute, I try to instil in him a feeling that he is inferior to none.'

From a marketing perspective, if a company's product is good and its founder has excellent storytelling skills, then the whole world not only listens but also helps spread the message. With his story, Anand has won the hearts of many people. Today, Anand is a well-renowned speaker with millions of fans. He has given lectures at many famous institutions, and his story has been the subject of documentaries.

Anand Kumar's abilities to simplify complex subjects and instil confidence through storytelling have changed the lives of many students. Additionally, his inspiring journey has created a lot of awareness about the abilities of students from underprivileged backgrounds and the transformational power of education.

> Nelson Mandela said, 'Education is the most powerful weapon which you can use to change the world.' When a child gets educated, then his home and the lives of his family members, and his future generations change forever.
>
> Super 30 has made a difference not just in the lives of its students and their families but also changed the mindset of people by giving them hope. Earlier, a driver would serve to keep his employer happy not just to ensure the continuation of his job but also with the hope that one day his son would be gainfully employed by the same employer. But now, looking at the examples of Super 30 alumni, the same driver can also see the dream of great education and a better life for his children.
>
> Anand says, 'Making quality education accessible to the masses will make a huge difference to the world by solving the core issues of poverty, unemployment, population explosion, environmental degradation, and a lot more.' To increase the scale of the impact he can make, now, Anand is working on teaching school students in various parts of the country through online channels. Furthermore, many of his former Super 30 students are supporting multiple educational initiatives. Undoubtedly, Anand's contribution can inspire many others to start similar initiatives for underprivileged students and help India achieve greater heights.

ANAND KUMAR

Advice from Anand Kumar

- The first aspect of creating any business is to win the trust of your customers. For winning trust, don't try to sell any high-priced product suddenly. Initially, start with a low-priced small product, so that people can try it without spending much. This small product will help in winning the trust of customers, and with time, new products can evolve.
- To build a great brand, an entrepreneur has to be a great leader. One of the prominent qualities of a great leader is to congratulate his team and give them credit for success, and when a failure occurs, the leader should own that failure.
- A big dream + a keen desire to succeed + positive thinking + continuous hard work + boundless patience is the simple arithmetic for success.
- You can achieve anything, no matter how big your goal is. All that is required is to have patience and hard work without getting distracted by adversity.

Quikr

Aasaan hai badalna

Making the invisible market visible

Dr A.P.J. Abdul Kalam once said, 'A door is much smaller compared to the house, a lock is much smaller compared to the door, and a key is the smallest of all but a key can open the entire house. Thus, a small, thoughtful solution can solve major problems.' With similar principles, in 2008, Pranay Chulet founded Quikr, which is solving the day-to-day problems of 30 million unique visitors who visit the platform every month.

The inception of this journey goes back to the time when Pranay was living in the USA. With a keen interest in films, he decided to learn filmmaking at the New York Film Academy, despite having spent a decade as a management consultant. As destiny would have it, in 2007, Pranay's passion turned him into filmmaker temporarily. He wrote an ambitious script with 30 characters for which he needed people of different nationalities. Pranay used Craigslist (an American classifieds website) to hire his cast and crew members, and within a week, he was able to audition 200 actors. Along with the USA, Pranay had planned some parts of the film to be shot in India. But in India, he couldn't find a one-stop digital classifieds solution like Craigslist.

Pranay says, 'Many things in life happen by serendipity rather than planning.' He had never planned to come back to India permanently, but his movie project kept on extending, and he spent more time in India than he had expected. During his stay, he always felt that a platform like Craigslist had a lot more potential in developing markets like India. Thinking about the impact he could make, Pranay decided to stay back to create India's answer to Craigslist.

In 2008, he started Quikr, which evolved to become India's largest classifieds platform. In 2015, Quikr organised itself into five verticals: QuikrBazaar, QuikrEasy, QuikrCars & Bikes, QuikrJobs and QuikrHomes. Later, the company went deeper into transactions and launched Quikr Assured. Now, besides being India's largest classifieds platform, Quikr also operates as India's largest transaction marketplace for pre-owned goods and services.

Within a decade, Quikr achieved phenomenal growth with its leadership position extending across traffic, listings, transactions, revenue as well as profitability status. It won recognition as India's most trusted classifieds brand and most trusted e-commerce brand by *The Economic Times*' Brand Equity Survey. Furthermore, for his notable achievements, Pranay received the Distinguished Alumnus Award from his alma mater IIM Calcutta.

Inspiringly, Quikr is one of the most valued startups in India. The company is backed by many leading investors, including Tiger Global Management, Kinnevik, Matrix Partners India, Omidyar Network, Norwest Venture Partners, Nokia Growth Partners, Warburg Pincus, Steadview Capital and eBay, among others.

This chapter covers the exciting journey of Quikr, one of the most popular internet brands in the country.

THE BEGINNING

Pranay was born into a middle-class family and grew up in Dariba, a mining town near Udaipur in Rajasthan. He was the first one from his school—Kendriya Vidyalaya (Dariba)—to ever appear in and clear the IIT entrance examination. After earning a BTech from IIT Delhi, Pranay graduated from IIM Calcutta with a gold medal, in 1996.

After completing his education, Pranay moved to New York, where he joined Mitchell Madison Group, a strategy consulting firm. After working with the group for almost three years, in 2000, he started his first venture, Reference Check, an online medium between service providers and consumers. The company eventually merged with Walker Digital.

Pranay then went on to work with Walker for a brief period to build and stabilise the business, thus earning himself a US patent in the area of matchmaking between buyers and sellers. Subsequently, as a Principal at Booz & Co. in New York, he helped large US media companies, including movie studios and publishers, evaluate and launch new digital businesses. In 2007, he started Excellere, a startup for web-based educational products.

In 2008, with a vision to provide a platform for sellers and buyers to meet virtually and transact offline, Pranay launched Quikr along with his friend Jiby Thomas (who left the company in 2012). The initial two to three years were very tough. Market sentiments were not great, and funding was almost unavailable because of the global financial crisis in 2008. During those days, startups were not a preferred career choice, which made hiring the right talent difficult. Furthermore, internet penetration was low, which made it difficult to get people to use the platform. Though its initial growth was gradual, Quikr, later, took the market by storm.

THE BRAND NAME: QUIKR

Building an online marketplace is an arduous task. It is like solving a chicken-and-egg mystery of who comes first: buyers or sellers. To get buyers, you need sellers, and to attract sellers, you need a lot of buyers. Pranay sensed that to stand out in today's noisy world, the brand name had to be catchy, and the platform had to be clear and fast.

Considering the nature of the business, he felt the name Quikr (which is a play on the word quicker) would be a perfect fit. Quikr is a memorable brand name and evokes thoughts of fast transactions between buyers and sellers. Fortunately, the domain name Quikr.com was available, and Pranay picked it up.

BUSINESS LESSONS

Many important business lessons can be learnt from the evolution of Quikr. A few of them are as follows.

Organise the unorganised

People no longer buy products for life, now they want to sell their furniture, mobiles, cars, etc., after using them for a while. At the same time, there is a huge demand for used goods from a bigger India that aspires to own but cannot afford expensive goods. Till platforms like Quikr appeared, people sold their old belongings through inefficient and ineffective solutions such as scrap dealers or newspaper classifieds. These avenues come with limitations of their own in terms of shelf life, reach and cost-effectiveness. For example, the same newspaper might not be read by buyers and sellers in different locations, and the cost of posting an advertisement in newspaper classifieds could be much higher than the revenue a seller would make. Also, the shelf life of a classified advertisement in a newspaper is just one day.

In such an unorganised market, Quikr positioned itself as a handshake platform where buyers and sellers could meet, chat, bargain and strike deals. Initially, Quikr started as a classic C2C (consumer-to-consumer) platform to connect buyers and sellers. With time, Quikr's B2C (business-to-consumer) model evolved to where businesses could transact with consumers. Via Quikr, many Indians in remote areas sell farm produce such as desi ghee and even mithai. In terms of social impact, Quikr helps small enterprises like tiffin services and travel agents grow their business. It also allows women entrepreneurs to launch their businesses and helps students locate educational opportunities and get employment.

Quikr's evolution has been part designed and part natural. Though Quikr started as a platform for buying and selling goods, people started using it for multiple purposes, like posting jobs, selling services, renting homes and so on. In 2015, Quikr reorganised its business around five verticals: QuikrHomes (digital real-estate business), QuikrCars & Bikes (a one-stop destination for car and bike buyers and sellers), QuikrJobs (connecting recruiters and job seekers for entry-level white-collar jobs and blue-collar jobs), QuikrBazaar (where users can buy and sell used goods) and QuikrEasy (an on-demand home services platform catering to 200 plus service requirements that range from pest control to appliance repair to interior designing). The power of a diversified platform like Quikr is that while it attracts consumers in one area, they end up using it for multiple adjacent areas as well.

Steve Jobs once said, 'I think if you do something and it turns out pretty good then you should go do something else wonderful, not dwell on it for too long. Just figure out what's next.' Quikr's team is always on the lookout for a new area to organise. For instance, India's secondhand market, which comprises mostly of vehicles and refurbished electronics, lacks transparency. This makes customers hesitant about choosing used products. To address this concern, Quikr launched Quikr Assured. All products in the Assured offerings are checked for quality and come with a full warranty from Quikr while all services are delivered by trained professionals, thus making transactions on Quikr 100 per cent secure and safe. Quikr also offers EMI options and faster delivery time on these products and services.

Conventionally, C2C transactions have been limited by geography. If one had to buy something secondhand, one would not travel far and wide to buy it. Secondly, these transactions were cash-dependent. To enable C2C buying and selling across India, Quikr launched Quikr Doorstep, which addresses genuine consumer issues of trust, payment and logistics. With Quikr's messaging platform, buyers and sellers can negotiate online, and with the Doorstep feature, buyers can make secure payments while sellers can use the pick-up and delivery facilities to ship goods directly to the buyer. For the safety of payments, the Doorstep feature provides an escrow account, which ensures that transactions are safe for buyers. Quikr transfers the money to the seller's account only when the buyer accepts the product, and in case of returns or cancellations, Quikr ensures that the buyer's money as well as the seller's product are returned.

By organising the unorganised market, Quikr has been able to create a lot of hidden value. Moreover, the rising internet penetration, usage of smartphones, and the evolving mindset of consumers have acted as catalysts in the exponential rise of Quikr. Today, the brand is present in over 1,200 cities with

30 million monthly users, 98 per cent of whom come to the platform organically.

Create a powerful brand identity

Pranay says, 'When we started, we were nobody, and we didn't have money for marketing.' Initially, the team focused all its energy on creating a simplified product. Interestingly, when Quikr started, there was an unmet need in the market. Newspapers charged money for their classifieds section, and Quikr was a free and easy-to-use platform, so people were ready to give it a try. When the product started becoming popular through word of mouth, the team decided to amplify the user base through digital marketing channels such as SEM (search engine marketing), retargeting and display networks.

Each medium has a role to play. Online marketing is a great way to make people try your product, but when you are building a mass brand, TV helps in establishing credibility. Quikr has a pan India presence in both urban and rural areas, and a large number of its potential consumers are not online but will be online in the future. So, after four years in business, when the user base needed a boost, and some funding had been raised, the company decided to invest in mass marketing channels, including print and television. During this period, Quikr put equal focus on digital and traditional mass media channels.

Quikr extended its presence across key social media channels such as Facebook, Twitter, Instagram and YouTube, with a carefully crafted content strategy. In terms of advertisements, Quikr fundamentally changed the rules of the game by consistently coming up with hilarious advertisements. For instance, in one of the advertisements, actor Murli Sharma (from *Singham*) is shown as a police inspector standing on a police jeep with a hand siren (bhopu). While trying to address rioters during a curfew, he abruptly states, '*Aur ek baat, main apne ghar ka saara saaman bech dena chahta hoon.*' In response, one of the rioters yells back, 'Quikr.com *pe bech na.*'

In India, IPL is the most popular sporting event. People even watch the auction of players ahead of IPL with great fascination. When in one season of the IPL, a few cricketers did not get picked in the auction, Quikr released three advertisements around this theme. Each advertisement started with actor Murli Sharma sitting beside a person facing his back to the camera with the player name written on his jersey and stating '*Yeh hai Gibbs* [player name]. *Ise 'IBL* [a take on IPL]' *mein kisine nahi khareeda. Lekin agar woh bike hota ...*' followed by the fake Gibbs metamorphosing into a bike named 'Gibbs' and the dialogue continues '*toh Quikr.com mein jhatt se bik jaata.*'

Quikr has an uncanny knack for understanding what kind of communication works with the viewers. When there was a match-fixing scandal that left the nation fretting, fuming and venting, Quikr took advantage of the conversations, adding to the interest in the topic, and riding the wave. A static ad appeared on Quikr's Facebook page within 36 hours of the news of the scandal breaking out, and the film appeared within 72 hours. The underlying concept of the ad was: 'Why sell yourself for money? If you want, sell something old from your house on Quikr.com.' Similarly, there were many other advertisements that not only made people smile but also made them realise the power of Quikr as a platform.

In 2014, Quikr partnered with youth events, including popular music festivals like Sunburn and Supersonic, and launched contests for free tickets on Twitter. To connect better with youngsters, Quikr teamed up with the youth platform All India Bakchod (AIB) and launched a few out-of-the-box humorous videos. The first online video *Mobile Bechna Hain?*

shows a customer who goes to a shop to sell his mobile phone but gets harried by the shopkeeper who offers to pay him a meager ₹54 for his six-month-old phone. It ends with the message 'Aise logon ke muhh kyun lagna? Find your perfect buyer only on Quikr.' The second video, *Quikr Date Film*, opens at a restaurant where a middle-class guy takes a girl out to an expensive restaurant. As the girl keeps selecting dishes and ordering them, the guy keeps on selling things on his Quikr mobile app. At the end, when the girl goes on to order desserts, the guy has no option left but to click his picture and put it up on Quikr with the message 'For sale: Good Friend, Forever Alone.' The video ends with the message 'The only place you'll never be undervalued.' Both of these videos clocked millions of views on YouTube.

Around 2014, Quikr increased its focus on TV, digital as well as traditional mass media channels. Just before Diwali, with the intent to influence the household purchases of viewers and aid in upgrading their items, Quikr partnered with Star Plus and appeared as a part of the storyline in serials with fairly good TRPs like *Veera*, *Nisha aur Uske Cousins* and *Saath Nibhaana Sathiya*. All these partnerships created high recall and generated sufficient conversations for the brand to get noticed, remembered and eventually used.

Till 2015, its logo was playful, and Quikr had the positioning of a casual classifieds brand. When the company decided to verticalise its business and go deeper into high-performing categories like jobs, homes, services, goods and autos, it decided to change the brand identity from casual to mature. In 2015, the new brand logo was launched with a new slogan, '*Aasan hai badalna*.' The company hired Bollywood actor Ranveer Singh and Kollywood (Tamil) actor Suriya as its brand ambassadors and launched TV campaigns promoting various features and verticals.

With the help of mass media campaigns, Quikr became a famous brand with charismatic recall. As the company realised a substantial rise in its user base, its marketing budget was equally divided between digital and TV. Influencers help in spreading the brand message with the right audience and in building mindshare for the brand. To reach out to its target audience, Quikr made influencer programmes a crucial part of its social media and digital strategy. Also, to touch consumers' daily lives and connect with them in person, Quikr continuously organised brand activation campaigns in residential complexes and malls in various cities. Quikr has also been running offline events in multiple cities. For instance, the Quikr Carfest, organised in Bengaluru, received footfall of more than 10,000 people. Car dealers turned the Carfest into an eye-catching event by driving in a host of drool-worthy supercars and luxury cars. With stunt bikers, live music and fun and food attractions, the Quikr Carfest had something for everyone. Also, a 7-feet-long quirky car made up of 2,000 mobile phones became a unique attraction. Moreover, five lucky winners got to meet and greet the movie star Suriya.

Marketing analytics is the core of every campaign at Quikr. So, no campaign goes out without stating the campaign's objectives, and its performance is continuously monitored. If required, corrective actions are taken like stopping or scaling the campaign or changing the channel mix or the media base, to ensure a successful return on investment. Furthermore, if the services are limited to 12–15 cities, then television is not used. Also, in a lot of categories like services or hyperlocal services, digital initiatives work better. The company also uses artificial intelligence to send relevant push notifications to customers. For example, users who are coming in to rent a home will need to paint and clean it, and so on. So, relevant notifications are sent to them at the appropriate time, thereby making optimal use of the cross-category nature of the platform that is unique to Quikr.

In terms of building the brand identity of Quikr, each marketing channel has played an important role. Television has the highest reach and creates maximum buzz. Digitals and events create engagement and facilitate two-way communication. And outdoor advertising acts as a reminder. Through its marketing campaigns centred on an innovative storytelling approach, the brand has built a strong identity and achieved a leading market share.

Break the status quo

In the words of Seth Godin, 'Organisations that destroy the status quo win. Whatever the status quo is, changing it gives you the opportunity to be remarkable.' Not once, not twice, but multiple times, Quikr has broken the status quo. For instance, Quikr was inspired by a highly successful American classifieds company—Craigslist—but in terms of execution, it followed a very Indian model.

Quikr started in the desktop era when emails and text messages were a prominent form of communication, and people were not used to smartphones and apps. Those days, classifieds used to send emails, but a lot of people in India were not internet savvy. A business like Quikr is driven by network effects, and it needs both buyers and sellers. If it doesn't have enough sellers, it will not get enough buyers and vice versa. To get more sellers, Quikr kept its platform free for posting ads. Knowing that Indians, especially those from low-income groups, love missed calls, Quikr started a missed call service. Using this service, people who want to sell their goods on Quikr but lack internet access can ring up the company's call centre or, instead, its 'missed call centre' where employees return the calls to save costs for customers and post ads on their behalf. Initially, many people laughed at this approach, but over time, this service created a lot of word-of-mouth publicity and increased Quikr's popularity.

India is a very value-conscious market, and both buyers and sellers are price-sensitive. Sellers want to get the best price for what they are selling and, at the same time, buyers want a reasonable price for what they are hoping to purchase. The problem with used-goods transactions is that no one knows what the right price is. To help sellers determine a reasonably accurate value for their used goods before posting an ad on the platform, Quikr launched the Maximum Sales Price (MSP) calculator, the first pricing guide in the country for pre-owned goods. Similar in concept to the Maximum Retail Price (MRP), the MSP model also helps buyers understand if they are getting a fair price for the used products that they wish to purchase. This service helps both parties make informed decisions rather than random ones.

Privacy was a major concern for both buyers and sellers, and many people were not comfortable sharing their phone numbers online. So, Quikr launched an instant messenger named Quikr Nxt, which enables real-time conversations between buyers and sellers. Quikr Nxt takes user privacy to the next level by providing sellers with the option of connecting with prospective buyers and vice versa without providing their contact numbers or email IDs. In another pioneering move, Quikr brought the convenience of e-commerce to C2C transactions via its Doorstep service. Quikr Doorstep revolutionised C2C buying and selling in India, making it the first and only platform to complete all steps of the transaction online across the country.

Mobile phones form one of the most desired categories on Quikr, but people are always afraid of the quality of used phones.

To remotely evaluate the condition and quality of mobile phones listed on the platform, Quikr launched QuikrScanner, a pioneering diagnostic app for mobile phones. Furthermore, to consistently innovate for its users, Quikr launched the Quikr Developer platform, which allows external developers to offer innovative services or products to Quikr's end users. As a part of this initiative, Quikr is making its Application Programming Interfaces (APIs) available publicly. This allows developers in India's fast-expanding internet ecosystem to build innovative apps on Quikr's platform by registering for free.

In another first move for the industry, Quikr has become the only horizontal classifieds platform that has verticalised its business. This has allowed Quikr to unlock a robust strategy of building transactional marketplaces across these verticals. Moreover, under Quikr Assured, the company has taken the responsibility of completing transactions for its customers in co-living, real-estate brokerage, cars and bikes, goods and beauty and home services. Both classifieds and transaction parts of the business are experiencing steep growth due to their symbiotic relationship.

By November 2019, Quikr had been growing at 100 per cent year-over-year for the past five years. Nearly half of India's population is online, and the spending power of India's millennials, who believe in building an environment-conscious economy by using digital, shared, rented and pre-owned goods, is growing. With these factors at play, the brand is expected to see a similar level of growth for the next several years.

Become a market leader, but stay nimble like a startup

Nike's founder Phil Knight said, 'It's alright to be Goliath but always act like David.' Every business starts small like David, and over time, a few startups emerge as market leaders like Goliath. Both market leaders and startups have their own strengths. Startups are agile, innovative, risk-taking and opportunistic. On the other hand, market leaders have resources, power, money, brand reputation, customers, systems and processes, and the ability to execute at scale. It's a great achievement for any startup to become one of the leaders in its respective industry. But sometimes, leaders get into their comfort zones, begin to feel proud of their market shares, and consequently miss out on emerging opportunities and threats to business growth. To avoid getting into a comfort zone, Pranay believes one should not get intoxicated with their own success and keep learning how to get better.

By 2015, Quikr had become a horizontal leader in the Indian classifieds market. Classifieds is a media business where people come on the platform because it's free, and advertisers meet revenue targets through advertisements and paid listings. But from an advertisement business perspective, India is not a big market like the USA, so Quikr had to create new revenue models. Being an ambitious company, Quikr decided to undergo a transactionalisation and verticalisation of its businesses. Under the same mother brand—Quikr—the company launched five offshoots: QuikrHomes, QuikrCars, QuikrJobs, QuikrBazaar and QuikrEasy. These verticals act as five separate business units within Quikr with their separate P&L targets and different revenue models around advertisements, paid listings, lead generation and transactions.

Because of its verticalised structure within a horizontal structure, the company has synergies of a horizontal structure in terms of brand, cross-selling and talent while also having the specialisation and flexibility of single-category verticals. This structure also helps the company manage the cost of its workforce. Some people work in one vertical, while those in functions like HR, admin, finance, product, marketing, etc. work across verticals. From a returns on investment (ROI) perspective, spends on marketing and resources can be recovered from five verticals instead of one. Pranay says, 'Though this restructuring has played a significant role in Quikr's growth, creating this structure was like moving a ship.' In 2015, to get access to talent, Quikr moved its base from Mumbai to Bengaluru. Due to the verticalisation of the business, the company went through a lot of internal restructuring along with a change in management. Also, due to a change in the direction of the business from a media to a transaction-based business, a lot of temporary challenges and naysayers appeared. But as the seeds of change were sown then, the organisation is able to reap the benefits now.

Though externally, Quikr may look like a single business, on the ground level, it caters to a diverse set of consumer needs across 180 categories in 1,200 cities. Furthermore, these cities are the collection of localities, and transactions happen at a local level. So, the business has to be built in a very local way. At any given time, a hundred different tests are running in a hundred different cities to understand users' priorities. Every city is different in Quikr. For instance, Udaipur will have open Jeeps for sale, towns in Punjab may have ploughs mounted on Royal Enfield bullet bikes, while a city like Kolkata might have women entrepreneurs advertising home-made puchkas (or panipuri)—all this is based on consumer behaviour in each city. While the platform primarily connects the users and providers of goods and services in local markets, its housing and job listings attract users from other markets as well.

To achieve its current size and scale, Quikr has grown both organically and inorganically through acquisitions. It has acquired 15 companies, including Babajob and Hiree in the jobs space;

Zimmber, Salosa, Zapluk and Stayglad in the home services space; India Property, HDFC Realty, HDFC Red, Indian Realty Exchange, Realty Compass, Grabhouse and CommonFloor in the realty space; Stepni in car-related services and Zefo in the goods space. For these acquisitions, Quikr's team identified startups that had a great product but were unable to scale their business because of the lack of a brand name and users. Quikr brought those models and plugged them into its supply and demand network. Now, 15 per cent of Quikr's revenue comes from acquired companies, 35 per cent from the models built using acquired companies, and the remaining half from the original platform. To highlight the success of Quikr's M&A strategy, Grabhouse is an excellent example to highlight. When Quikr acquired this real-estate startup, it had a great product but just 600–800 tenants, and today, under the umbrella of Quikr, it has catered to over 1,00,000 tenants. This growth has happened without any marketing because there is already a lot of supply and demand for shared rentals on Quikr.

When a company starts growing fast, it becomes hard to maintain the same level of quality that it had as a small company with a small team. People get intoxicated with numbers-driven growth and start forgetting the organisation's core values and the need to focus on user experience. But Quikr didn't face that challenge because Pranay identified this issue before it became a cause of alarm for the company.

As Quikr is growing in terms of its size and reputation, its responsibility towards its users is also increasing. Over time, the quality of listings has become more important than the number of listings. Suboptimal listings are deleted through technology and human intervention so that quality doesn't get lost in the noise. At the same time, to connect millions of buyers with the right sellers, the company has built matchmaking algorithms.

Pranay says, 'Though we've become larger, we've worked very hard to stay flexible, fast-moving and frugal like a startup. We still are more a walk-and-talk kind of place rather than the long-meetings type, and that's how we like it.' He ends by saying, 'It would be particularly uncool for us to turn into some slow-moving monolithic machine as we grow. Our very name is Quikr.'

Create a high-performance work culture

Airbnb's founder Brian Chesky said, 'A company's culture is the foundation for future innovation. An entrepreneur's job is to build the foundation.' An organisation's culture defines what is encouraged, discouraged, accepted or rejected there. Since the initial days of Quikr, Pranay has focused on setting the right foundation for the company's culture.

A company's culture is formed by its people. And it is the people that drive it further. According to Pranay, internet companies are analytics companies at heart. So, he has a strong orientation towards hiring analytical people who enjoy answering the puzzles presented in the interviews. In fact, Quikr's interview process requires even C-level executives to solve puzzles and analytical problems. This helps in understanding how good they are with numbers and structured thinking. At Quikr, every person involved in the hiring process is trained on aspects that the company looks for in a candidate. Moreover, in determining the right people, Quikr places great weightage on character attributes. Pranay says, 'Building a company is a marathon and not a sprint, so you want to work with people you enjoy working with.' While hiring people, Quikr also looks for softer aspects like loyalty, commitment and how excited the applicant is to work at the company.

The many companies that Quikr acquired came with a lot of talent. Sometimes the acquiring company shows arrogance towards people from the acquired company, but Pranay thinks giving respect to talent is winning half the battle. When employees get respect, they become passionate about the values and the core mission of the organisation. Once the freshly acquired become dedicated to accomplishing the same goal as the company that acquired them, it becomes easier to absorb them within the organisational structure.

Culture brings people together as a team. Pranay believes that though a single person starts a company, it takes effort on part of many people to scale it up. Being a diversified platform, Quikr has different business units that are headed and run by many talented people. Pranay looks at them as partners building a great company. He considers every employee, every agency, every media planner, every business alliance and every brand ambassador a partner who has directly or indirectly helped in making the company what it is today.

With its focus on innovations, at any given point in time multiple experiments are going on within Quikr. Pranay believes in a pilot fast, scale fast approach. But he is also clear that teams have to be intellectually honest. If something is not working, then it has to be stopped to cut any further time or resource losses. Employees make hundreds of decisions on their own every day, and the company's culture is their guide. Quikr attempts to inculcate a data-driven culture. Though higher-level decisions are sometimes based on gut, everyday decisions at the company are backed by data rather than being based on assumptions.

Focus on customer orientation sets the culture of one company apart from another. Pranay comes from a small town and has seen the simplistic way of Indian life. He thinks that often people appreciate the power of technology but miss out on the point of view of their users, many of whom have not even experienced the internet. He always pushes his teams to think from the users' point of view rather than the digital point of view.

Most people believe a brand is created by its logo and design, marketing and advertising, external communications and the way a company presents itself at various touchpoints. But a powerful brand is far more than that. For a brand to be authentic, the journey starts from within the company. The people behind the brand are the most critical brand assets, as everything that comes from the brand begins with them. Quikr's focus on creating a high-performance work culture is a definite competitive advantage that keeps the company ahead in a highly crowded and competitive market.

Paulo Coelho's masterpiece *The Alchemist* tells the mystical story of Santiago, a shepherd boy who desires to travel in search of a worldly treasure. His quest leads him to riches far different and far more satisfying than he ever imagined. This story is a representation of the transforming power of our dreams, people in our lives, and the importance of listening to our hearts.

Similar to this story, when Pranay had left India for a promising career in the USA, he had not imagined that the universe had its own plans for him. His hobby of filmmaking brought him to India and helped connect him to a larger purpose in life. He listened to his heart and stayed in India to follow his dream. Eventually, he created one of the most respected internet brands in the country—Quikr.

PRANAY CHULET

Advice from Pranay Chulet

- If you want to start a company, the only way to do is to start it. It is essential to have a sense of the direction that you are going in and the business that you want to build, but it is equally vital to not overanalyse things because every business evolves.
- It is best to keep things simple in the initial stages of business; if you have too many moving parts, then too many things need to fall in line for you to make a beginning. Rather than thinking about how you will conquer the world, it is essential to figure out the smallest part of the market and then go from there.
- Nothing will teach you more than your market itself. So, don't go for perfection initially. First, launch something that can be used by a few users, and what they tell you is more important than anything else.
- Don't ever get into a business with a 'get rich quick' attitude because life doesn't come with a planned lottery. You need to be prepared for the long run.
- Have fun today in whatever you are doing! Sometimes people do multiple things in life, considering that those things would look good on their resume and keep delaying the thing that they really want to do. As Warren Buffet said, it's like saving up sex for your old age. So, get into something that you would love to do.

OYO

Reinventing hospitality

Steve Jobs, a college dropout from America, inspired the whole world by creating the most valuable company on the planet—Apple. He often said, 'Your time is limited, so don't waste it living someone else's life. Don't be trapped by dogma—which is living with the results of other people's thinking. Don't let the noise of others' opinions drown out your own inner voice. And most importantly, have the courage to follow your heart and intuition.' Many might have just read it, but one young man followed this statement and revolutionised the hospitality ecosystem for ever. Ritesh Agarwal followed his heart and intuition in such an unconventional manner that most people would have called it madness. He dropped out of college but went on to create the fastest-growing hospitality chain on the planet—OYO Hotels & Homes.

Founded in 2013 with just one hotel in Gurgaon, OYO has quickly emerged as the largest hotel chain in India. Beyond India, OYO operates multiple brands of hotels (budget, mid-market and upscale), homes, living spaces, co-working spaces, leisure resorts, wedding venues and other hospitality areas in countries like China, Malaysia, Nepal, the UK, the USA, the UAE, Saudi Arabia, the Philippines, Indonesia, Vietnam and Japan. By September 2019, OYO had become the world's third-largest hotel chain.

Today, Ritesh is considered one of the youngest founders in the world. His journey started early. At the age of 19, he became the first resident Indian and also the first person from Asia to win the prestigious Thiel Fellowship, set up by Peter Thiel, the co-founder of PayPal, the first major investor of Facebook and a legend in his own right. Over the years, Ritesh has received numerous awards, including *Forbes* 30 under 30, *Fortune* 40 under 40, *The Economic Times* 40 under 40, CNBC's Young Turk of the Year, EY Entrepreneur of the Year, *Forbes* Tycoons of Tomorrow, NDTV Dream Chaser of the Year and many more.

According to media reports, OYO has raised a significant amount of funding from marquee investors, including Lightspeed Venture Partners, Sequoia India, Greenoaks Capital, SoftBank Vision Fund, the Chinese ridesharing and transportation giant Didi and the world's largest home-sharing platform Airbnb. This chapter discusses the inspiring journey of OYO Hotels & Homes, one of the most popular Indian brands in the world.

THE BEGINNING

Ritesh was born and brought up in a middle-class Marwari family, a community well-known for its business acumen, in Bissamcuttack, a small town in the Rayagada district of Odisha. With an innate curiosity to learn, he began software programming at the early age of eight! Initially, he wanted to become an aircraft pilot. Then, one day, he heard the word 'entrepreneur' from his elder sister who had gone to an entrepreneurship festival.

Curious to know what the word meant, Ritesh referred to a dictionary and found that an entrepreneur is someone who solves a problem and creates a business by doing so. After that, whenever his teachers asked him what he wanted to be when he grew up, Ritesh's answer would be: entrepreneur. He was so enthusiastic and driven that at the age of 13, he started selling SIM cards and FMCG products. Because he was a brilliant student, by the time Ritesh was in Class X, his parents decided to send him to Kota to prepare for the IIT entrance exam. In 2009, Ritesh started attending Bansal Tutorials in Kota. As he was away from his home, he had a lot of time to do just about anything he wanted. So, he did something that no other student had done—he wrote a book called *The Encyclopaedia of Indian Engineering Colleges*. This book turned out to be a massive hit on Flipkart at the time. Soon, living in Kota and preparing for the IIT entrance exam began to bore him. He started travelling to Delhi to attend entrepreneurship events. As he couldn't afford the registration costs, Ritesh would often just sneak in. Through these events he was able to glimpse larger ambitions.

Because many students spent their time preparing for the IIT entrance exam, his school in Kota was not strict about attendance. So, Ritesh started working for entrepreneurs in Delhi and went back to Kota only to give exams. As Kota is very far from his hometown, Ritesh's parents were not aware of Ritesh's travels and shift of focus for a long time. Fortunately, he scored well enough in his school exams to pacify his family.

After Class XII, Ritesh moved to Delhi and got admitted to a college, only to drop out three days later to start his own business. It was difficult for him to convince his parents about the decision he had taken. However, Ritesh was aware that as an entrepreneur he would need to convince many people, and convincing his parents was just the beginning. He told them that many students take a gap year between school and college to prepare for competitive exams, and he wanted to do the same—but to work on his business idea. He assured his parents, if things didn't work out, he would join college again. With his perseverance, Ritesh made things work for him, and he has not looked back since then.

THE BRAND NAME: OYO

During his travels from Kota to Delhi, Ritesh had realised that there was a massive gap between the demand and the supply of budget hotels. To make small hotels, bed-and-breakfasts and inns more accessible to budget travellers, he launched Oravel Stays. He made a list of properties for this, but unfortunately, they received very few bookings and the repeat rate was very low. When he inquired, he found that customers were not happy with the experience at those hotels. To understand the pain points and expectations of travellers, he decided to travel for three months and stay at various small hotels, lodges and similar options.

Over a period of four months or so, he stayed in more than 100 bed-and-breakfasts, guest houses and small hotels across the country. During this period, he noticed numerous problems, including ramshackle buildings, missing signage, leaky washrooms, torn mattresses, stained floors, sputtering air-conditioning, non-acceptance of credit cards, rude staff and so on. Through this experience, he realised that the real problem was not the availability of hotels, but the inconsistency of the experience.

Meanwhile, Ritesh applied for the prestigious Thiel Fellowship. The Thiel Foundation awards $1,00,000 to 20 people under the age of 20 who have dropped out of college to start a business. Furthermore, the foundation provides resources to establish a startup and mentorship from the foundation's network of tech entrepreneurs, investors and scientists. This includes the likes of Facebook founder Mark Zuckerberg, Google founder Larry Page, Tesla founder Elon Musk and Peter Thiel himself.

Ritesh's ideas of transforming the hospitality industry at a global level got him the scholarship. He was the first Indian resident to receive this fellowship and his experience as a Thiel Fellow in Silicon Valley was pivotal to his understanding of the startup ecosystem. Being directly mentored by Peter Thiel was an invaluable experience for him. After coming back to India, Ritesh used the money received from the fellowship to improve upon the idea of Oravel. In 2013, he started OYO, a hospitality chain, with the belief that everyone deserves a beautifully designed, chic and comfortable living space, and a better life.

BUSINESS LESSONS

There are many important business lessons that can be learnt from the evolution of OYO Hotels & Homes. Let's elaborate on a few.

Start small, nail it, then make it big

One of the key things that Ritesh learnt from the Thiel Fellowship was that companies that want to start doing everything end up doing nothing. It is far wiser to start small, crack a specific market, and then begin scaling up across regions, product categories and customer segments.

With OYO, Ritesh started small. He approached Rajesh Yadav, the owner of a Gurgaon-based hotel that had almost zero occupancy. He asked Rajesh to allow him to brand, standardise and run the hotel for six months. The owner, desperate for business, allowed Ritesh to transform the hotel, as a part of

OYO, as long as Ritesh could guarantee a profit and bear any investment and loss. Ritesh played all roles in this one hotel—from housekeeping staff to sales and CEO. He experimented with innovative technologies and upgraded everything in the hotel, including linen, toiletries, bathroom fittings and Wi-Fi. He spent months in this hotel, and with his dedication and determination, the hotel's occupancy increased substantially.

In India, many people run small hotels as a side business. They don't have the right tools and technology needed to run a hotel, and they struggle to meet their occupancy targets. Moreover, a lot of these hotel owners want to invest their money, but they don't know what to do. By looking at the turnaround of that one hotel, many hotel owners approached Ritesh to give a miracle touch to their hotels. Months of hard work at one hotel had prepared Ritesh to take up more opportunities.

Within the next few months, OYO expanded to several hotels in Gurgaon and miraculously achieved over 80 per cent occupancy—a big thing for a place like Gurgaon. The foundation of this rapid growth was the OYO team's ability to bring its successful model of combining design, hospitality, technological expertise, financial acumen and operational capabilities for real-estate owners from around the world. By giving owners the ability to get a higher return on their investments, access financing opportunities to transform their hotels and offer excellent customer service, OYO was able to increase occupancy and profitability in each one of them.

OYO's business model consists of acquiring hotels and homes, on franchise, manchise or lease, renovating them, and bringing them up to OYO's standards. They do this by using technology and operational capabilities. This process ensures seamless management of the property in terms of revenue, pricing and the day-to-day experience of the guests. Then OYO uses an omnichannel distribution strategy to create demand. By May 2015, OYO had grown to become the largest budget hotel chain in India. In a short period, this makeover of standalone establishments by OYO not only helped hotel owners run a better show but fostered trust in the budget hotel industry. Owners of budget hotels had started looking up to OYO as a brand that takes accountability of not only improving the infrastructure but also training the staff and maintaining the upkeep of the property on a day-to-day basis. And then, what Ritesh had always wanted happened. Budget travellers started looking up to OYO as a brand that provided quality-assured accommodation at an affordable price.

Ritesh says, 'One big learning from Thiel Fellowship was to think really big and create an impact, without thinking if anybody has done it before.' While OYO's growth and impact continued in India, Ritesh decided to expand into international markets. Within a short span of six years, the organisation achieved what other brands in the hospitality sector took ages to achieve. OYO became India and South Asia's largest, China's second-largest and the world's third-largest fastest-growing chain of hotels, homes, managed living and workspaces. By September 2019, OYO had more than 1 million rooms across 23,000 hotels and over 1,25,000 holiday homes in over 800 cities in 80 countries. Moreover, every month, the company adds over 80,000 new rooms worldwide. Every night 5,00,000 heads rest on OYO pillows, which is a testament to the impact the brand is creating globally.

Surround yourself with the smartest of people

During the course of his Thiel Fellowship, Ritesh learnt that it is crucial to have the smartest of people around you, those who can be great leaders too. He says, 'Bringing people on board who consider themselves to be the CEO of whatever work they do is the foundation of building a brilliant company.'

An IIT and BHU alumnus, Anuj Tejpal was among the first to join Ritesh on his entrepreneurial journey. With Anuj as the chief business development officer, Ritesh was able to expand OYO's presence in Gurgaon. There was demand from customers, and hotel owners were ready to hand over their hotels, but OYO didn't have the staff to manage so many properties. Ritesh discussed his challenge with Bejul Somaia, partner at Lightspeed Ventures, the first institutional investor in OYO. Bejul told him that bringing one right person could change the fortune of a company. He told Ritesh that the best CEOs spend 40 per cent of their time meeting great people and bringing them on board and then letting them do what they want to do.

Initially, OYO's image was of being a real-estate business, which made it difficult for the company to get engineers on board. Ritesh went to Bengaluru to meet potential employees and tried to make them understand that OYO was a technology-driven company. He managed to convince them and flew back with three or four engineers. To hire people at senior positions, Ritesh decided to make use of LinkedIn. While a few people came forward to meet him, they didn't take him seriously because of his young age and education.

Eventually, Abhinav Sinha (chief operating officer), a Harvard MBA with experience at ITC and BCG, joined OYO. He brought critical experience in organisational redesign from his consulting experience. And then there was no looking back. Leaders like Abhishek Gupta (the chief financial officer), an ISB alumnus with a lengthy finance career at GE and Philips; Ayush Mathur (the chief supply officer), an ISB alumnus with experience at ITC; Kavikrut (the chief growth officer), a

Harvard MBA; Maninder Gulati (the chief strategy officer), an ISB alumnus with experience at Lightspeed Ventures, McKinsey and ITC; and Dinesh Ramamurthi (the chief human resources officer), an alumnus of TISS with experience at companies like ITC and Coca-Cola came on board.

As the company was growing rapidly, it needed executives to juggle multiple functions and demands from both the consumer and the supplier's sides, especially with anything related to supply chains, logistics and manpower. Ritesh asked his leadership team to suggest the smartest people they have worked with. Then from their network, many people with valuable experiences from across some of the biggest manufacturing and retail companies in India and abroad were hired. Over time, OYO has hired numerous executives who drive different areas of business in different regions. Interestingly, Ritesh is the only dropout among his team, and he is heading a team of leaders from IIMs, IITs, Harvard and Ivy League colleges with rich industry experience.

Ritesh is a prolific learner, who sets the pace from the top. He says, 'At OYO, I call myself the chief clarity officer. This means that my job is to share what to do and advise what not to do. So, setting out the principles which enable everybody to decide how they can do their jobs.' Getting the top brains together and then getting them to work together are two different things. Ritesh says, 'Teams that share a strong camaraderie and are bound together by the same vision will enable a startup to grow and become sustainable.' So, he has focused on building a strong workplace culture from the beginning. He has created a 'listening culture' that encourages everyone to share their opinions. At the same time, he understands that the biggest leverage he can get out of the senior team he has put together is to let them run their own show.

Taking inspiration from other successful companies, Ritesh has deployed a distributed leadership model at OYO, which makes the organisation democratic in its functioning. Distributed leadership is about delegating decision-making to a broader group; letting employees own the problems you want them to solve; empowering leaders to own and drive parts of the organisation while retaining a strong management core. Interestingly, because of this approach, OYO has been able to stay agile and responsive in a fast-changing business environment.

With thousands of young people full of energy working across different departments, OYO, as a company, is driven by millennials. What Ritesh has witnessed and learnt about the young generation is that they want to work for a vision, which is more than just two meals a day. They look for ownership to make decisions, be accountable and create an impact. Under Ritesh's leadership, OYO has established a team of thousands of employees and partners who are dubbed 'OYOpreneurs' and are encouraged to take ownership of their own projects. Most importantly, the company regularly highlights stories of OYOpreneurs who are driving the company's success.

Interestingly, OYO hasn't lost a single senior leader in the past six years, and Ritesh counts this as a crucial factor behind the company's exponential growth, which is seldom seen in contemporary companies where attrition of employees is a huge problem. Interestingly, LinkedIn ranked OYO the number one startup to work for in India, in 2018 as well as 2019.

Challenge the status quo and dare to do something new

George Bernard Shaw said, 'The reasonable man adapts himself to the world. The unreasonable one persists in trying to adapt the world to himself. Therefore, all progress depends on the unreasonable man.' On similar lines, Ritesh disrupted the hospitality industry by empowering small and independent hotel owners to compete with big hotel chains.

Mainstream hospitality brands like Marriott, Starwood, The Oberoi, Taj Hotels, Hyatt and others provide a consistent experience and are popular amongst the premium or luxury market segments. They constitute around 20 per cent of the hotel supply in the world. Eighty per cent of hotel assets in the world are unbranded, unorganised, unrated, or one- or two-star hotels. The budget market segment prefers these hotels. Unfortunately, many budget hotels don't even meet the fundamental needs of a budget traveller. For decades, budget travellers had been facing a problem of finding predictable experiences at the right price point.

Ritesh believed that he could change the way people live in every sense. He did that by upgrading bland and generic places into desirable living spaces and offering them at hard-to-ignore prices. That's how OYO (now known as OYO Hotels & Homes) was launched in May 2013.

Innovation continues to be a key growth driver and competitive advantage for OYO. The company lays a lot of emphasis on technology—something that the traditional chains have consistently lagged in embracing. It has an in-house stack of proprietary technology powering 20 plus applications for all stakeholders, including employees, customers and asset owners. OYO has the technology to help its internal workforce manage both the supply and the demand efficiently. Traditional hotel chains typically take around 10 months to sign a franchise or management contract deal with a property owner. But using technology, OYO usually signs a deal within 10 days of first meeting with a property owner.

OYO OS (operating system) is the next-generation system of hotel management. Every hotel that is part of the OYO chain of hotels works on the OYO OS, giving the cutting-edge advantage of sophisticated features, including express check-in and check-out. This operating system allows online procurement and inventory management and offers apps for housekeeping and audits while introducing solutions for multiple hotel management aspects like expense management, staff training and engagement, along with performance reviews and incentives for the hotel staff. After identification, the process of auditing and standardising hotels before making them live begins. The transformation app, OYO Optimus, enables teams to understand the transformation requirements, assign tasks, track progress and so on. It also enables overall visibility of the process to all the respective stakeholders, including the hotel owner and the OYO team.

To offer an enhanced customer experience, OYO's team uses Krypton, an internal audit app, to audit the properties. During the initial years, the audits were done physically, as they still are in many hotels, limiting the number of rooms and hotels that are being audited. Now, with the technology that Krypton has brought, a single OYO Captain can manage the audit of over 300 rooms while improving the guest experience at the same time.

OYO's pricing, inventory allocation and revenue management are driven by a machine learning-based algorithm. The algorithm makes 60 million micro-optimisations, every day, to arrive at the optimal price point that ensures an affordable stay for guests while driving higher yields and occupancy across the 23,000 buildings that are a part of OYO's chain. It allows each hotel to drive maximum revenue per available room (RevPAR) based on its micro-location. Based on supply and demand, the algorithm can adjust the pricing dynamically. In peak times, pricing changes to deliver high RevPAR, and in low times, it goes down to allow maximum customers to experience the hotel while increasing profits for owners.

OYO leverages innovative technology to continuously improve guest experience. Through artificial intelligence and machine learning, the team looks at multiple metrics from the time of day, weather, location down to local events. This helps in learning precisely what kind of room a customer prefers, and what search results the customer is most likely to appreciate. Additionally, data science and analytics help the team predict customer behaviour, understand the customer lifetime value, and improve the guest experience at every step in a streamlined manner. The company is now deploying internet-of-things (IoT), in pilot mode, in a large number of rooms, which will help control things like AC temperature and lighting. Based on the captured data, the team will learn the temperature and lighting the guests prefer and auto-set the same before the guests check in.

OYO is the first company anywhere in the hospitality sector in the world to introduce technology-based solutions on the hoteliers' side to help them manage end-to-end operations. Independent hotel owners, mainly from the economy segment, can handle all daily functions of the property, such as bookings visibility, sales channels, customers' requests, housekeeping and finances with OYO's CO-OYO app without even interacting with the company staff. Through the CO-OYO app, asset owners can have complete visibility of cash flows, business performance, pricing, customer reviews and recommendations. The app includes advanced analytics, which enable a deep dive into asset performance over time. Its intuitive interface is easy to navigate as that is the most important thing for people who are not tech-savvy. Further, it boosts performance by providing insights and easy-to-understand metrics and graphs that allow the daily monitoring of performance.

For customers, the OYO app offers multiple functions in addition to booking rooms. These include room service for food and beverages, booking a cab and searching nearby restaurants. On the check-in day, the guest gets the details of the captain—OYO's local representative at the hotel—for any local assistance, thus ensuring 24X7 on-the-ground support. Leveraging technology, OYO has been able to deliver a great hospitality experience, which has helped scale-up its business rapidly.

One of the game changers in OYO's case has been flexible timing. When the team heard from guests that one of the biggest points of discomfort while booking a hotel is the lack of flexibility of check-in time, OYO launched the sunrise check-in feature that allows its guests the flexibility of choosing their check-in time, which can be as early as 6 a.m. OYO also provides a complimentary insurance package to its guests for protection against accidental death, baggage loss, unforeseen medical expenses, amongst other benefits such as OPD treatment, and so on, for the entire duration of their stay at an OYO property. Thus, OYO has set many new benchmarks in the hospitality industry. As a testament to its popularity, today, approximately 90 per cent of OYO's business comes from repeat and word-of-mouth customers.

Marketing is a necessary part of growth

Seth Godin said, 'Marketing is a contest for people's attention.' When OYO began, the biggest challenge was to direct traffic to the associate hotels, because if they did not get traffic, they would have pulled out and the entire model would have flopped. OYO is a mass brand but a large part of its audience is not tech-savvy.

Yet, at the same time, the brand has to register in the minds of all age groups.

To start with youngsters and then society as a whole, the team made OYO's presence felt across a lot of college campuses and partnered with wedding planners, event managers, convention centres and banquet halls. To engage millennials, OYO capitalised on digital marketing and built a vast and loyal following on various social media platforms. To connect with its audience at a deeper level, the team created multiple short videos and films. One of the videos, *Independence Day*, which featured Bollywood actors Manoj Bajpai and Raveena Tandon, fetched over a million views for the brand. Furthermore, OYO launched multiple short films that depicted travellers expressing themselves freely in the comfort of a hotel room. The brand also launched a high-impact online campaign #oneforeveryone, encouraging consumers to share their quirky hotel moments.

To bring traffic to the OYO app and create viewer engagement, OYO partnered with the reality show *MTV Roadies*, which is extremely popular among the youth. While the contestants of the show enjoyed the best hospitality experience at OYO, the brand ran an OYO Roadies contest on its app. Five lucky winners got the opportunity to meet the show's famous host—Bollywood actor and celebrity Rannvijay Singha—and win many exciting prizes. The campaign involved a 360-degree marketing approach where the contest was promoted via paid media (TV and Voot), owned media (CRM, banners on the OYO app) and social media platforms, and earned media (PR). The campaign led to a significant increase in performance metrics, like contest participation, a high click-through rate of push notifications and social media engagement.

To target user bases in different parts of the country that are not exposed to the *MTV Roadies* kind of content, the company runs many localised marketing activities. As an example, the team created bright red paper cups that would resonate with OYO's logo. Every custom paper cup distributed ran with the slogan 'Book an OYO in 3 Sips', and urged the beverage drinker to download the mobile app. These branded paper cups were distributed in shopping malls, corporate offices, colleges, railways and bus stands. Also, the company runs the OYO Brand Ambassador programme, in which selected college students create awareness within their circles, run campaigns in the college, manage hospitality for their college events, and bring in bookings for OYO. In the process, they gain essential skills in marketing, communication and leadership.

To increase its brand visibility and transaction, OYO has created exciting partnerships with over 2,500 brands, which are mission-oriented like OYO and have high user traffic. For example, OYO has partnered with SARVA, one of the most promising yoga and wellness startups. It is funded by an illustrious list of global investors, which include names like global pop icon Jennifer Lopez, Bollywood diva Malaika Arora and American baseball legend Alex Rodriguez. SARVA has set up wellness studios at select OYO Townhouses to enrich the wellness experiences of every customer. OYO has also partnered with ZEE5, India's fastest-growing OTT platform. Through this partnership, OYO offers its customers fantastic discounts on a ZEE5 subscription, and ZEE5 subscribers enjoy discounts when booking rooms via OYO.

Similarly, OYO has partnered with Airtel and Amazon Pay to launch OYO Stores on the Airtel Thanks app and Amazon Pay that enable the customers to book quality and affordable accommodations. On similar lines, OYO is creating some great campaigns with its partners and offering integrated services to travellers. OYO has also extended its offerings through its partners like MakeMyTrip in India and Ctrip in China.

OYO has multiple brands. To offer the right brand to the right customer segment, the team relies on a data science system for proper segmentation and targeting. This process helps reach the right set of customers with targeted messages. Every campaign is customised based on audience needs, preferences, platforms and business goals. The team continually keeps experimenting with different segments and takes customers' feedback on whether they like the brand's communication and product offering. This feedback eventually feeds the company's marketing, product and customer experience strategy.

Ritesh says, 'Every overnight success is a five- to ten-year-old journey.' Over the years, OYO has invested in building relationships with their stakeholders, like customers, asset owners, partners, influencers (including YouTubers and bloggers) and journalists by following three core principles—transparency, mutual respect and, above all, reminding each other that they are in this ecosystem for the long run. The stakeholders have not only appreciated the great product and services OYO is offering, but have also shared constructive feedback when required. Starting from Ritesh, OYO's global team is always on top of things. It owns relationships and nurtures them. Today, the word of mouth of customers, influencers, partners and earned media contributes a lot to OYO's growth. By September 2019, OYO had hosted over 11 million guests with a 90 per cent repeat rate.

Never stop evolving

J.P. Morgan said, 'Go as far as you can see; when you get there, you'll be able to see farther.' OYO's journey is a testament to this statement. Neither Ritesh nor his leadership team had a background in either the real-estate or the hospitality industry, but they identified problems and kept learning through execution. When the OYO team entered different cities, different countries and different cultures, they learnt, unlearnt and relearnt many things. By translating these learnings into actions quickly, OYO has been able to sustain its speed, scale and impact.

A lot of times, the secret is not doing new things but doing regular things very well, every day. Many of the innovations that OYO has brought were initially innovative work-arounds, but then the team created strong processes around them. Eventually, playbooks were created for onboarding properties, creating demand, and managing and auditing properties according to OYO standards. Even a new team member can refer to these playbooks and scale-up properties in new markets. Ritesh says, 'At OYO, we have invested a lot of our time in designing, building and perfecting our processes and systems. We like to call it—creating science out of art.' Moreover, to train its employees, the company runs 27 skill institutes globally.

For continual engagement of loyal customers and top-performing hotel owners, OYO has launched various initiatives. For instance, to recognise and reward frequent customers, OYO has launched OYO Wizard, a benefit membership programme that aims to deepen and strengthen customer relationships by providing highly rated and curated hotels to loyal guests at good prices. To offer exclusive benefits and opportunities to top-performing hotel owners for their personal and professional advancement, they launched the OYO Partner Engagement Network (OPEN). With exclusive retention incentives, partner benefits and financial support, the programme creates an ecosystem that helps asset owners thrive.

OYO aims to provide a standardised experience to people across the country when they are away from home. For its international expansion, the company doesn't blindly copy its India strategy. The most critical part of international expansion is building exceptional local leaders and teams. In every new market, the company takes care of localisation. For example, in Saudi Arabia, each room has an arrow to indicate the direction of Mecca to help the travellers pray.

OYO's ability to standardise offerings in mid-tier properties, brand them the right way, increase traffic through online acquisition, and boost occupancy rates follows a model that can be applied in other places too. Utilising these powerful capabilities as the foundation, OYO is diversifying not just in the hotel and homes market but has curated new offerings for the changing needs and the multiple segments of the modern-day traveller.

As the OYO brand name is primarily recognised as a budget accommodation provider, to change this stereotype and construct a fresh image in the mind of consumers which will be distinct from budget properties, the company has created multiple sub-brands such as OYO Townhouse (design-led accommodation), OYO Home (beautiful private homes in great locations), OYO LIFE (long-term rental offerings), Silver Key (service apartments), Capital O (corporate and executive hotel brand), Palette (upper-end leisure resorts) and others. Each sub-brand has its own unique identity and offerings, but the core promise of providing quality living spaces to everyone from travellers to householders remains the same throughout.

To gain significant momentum, OYO has acquired several brands. For instance, to enter into the wedding space, it has acquired Weddingz.in, India's largest wedding banquet company. To expand into the co-working spaces, which is the demand of the day for the Indian startup ecosystem, OYO acquired Innov8. To deepen its presence in Europe, OYO acquired the

Amsterdam-based vacation rental company @Leisure Group that operates brands like Belvilla, DanCentre and Danland. As a strategy, OYO looks at acquisition targets for the core capabilities they have created, and not just for market share.

Ritesh sincerely believes that OYO has just scratched the surface of the potential that it can tap. There are over 3.2 billion middle-income people around the world. OYO's mission is to upgrade all forms of real estate and thereby enable these middle-income travellers and city-dwellers to experience living the good life. With time, the marketplace will continue to change, technology will continue to develop, and the brand, OYO, will continue to evolve, as evolution is what leads to growth.

Ritesh recognised a fortunate business opportunity and developed a simplified solution—OYO—for millions of people looking for trusted and predictable hospitality experiences. Today, OYO Hotels & Homes has come a long way and is considered an iconic and innovative global brand from India.

Ritesh says, 'Complacency and arrogance can destroy the best of the brands. Staying humble and hungry is crucial to continued success.' So, instead of resting on its success and laurels, the OYO team is restless to create better experiences for every customer, every day at every property.

RITESH AGARWAL

Advice from Ritesh Agarwal

- Something I truly believe is that an entrepreneur should be willing to be hands-on during execution, especially in the early days of a startup. It is important to know how things work, ground up.
- Too many young entrepreneurs give up on their ambitions too early before they can make an impact. Perseverance is an irreplaceable trait, and one needs to keep going and putting in effort.
- As a startup scales, an entrepreneur should be able to identify talent both within the organisation and externally, and partner with the right leaders to support him and take over specific responsibilities. His role then is to have clarity about where he is headed and the direction the company needs to take for the long term.
- It is extremely important to build something that 100 people absolutely love using rather than make something that 1,000 people would just kind of like.

PORTEA

HEAL AT HOME

Delivering healthcare services to your doorstep

The financial health of a country is firmly dependent on the health and wellness of its citizens. Being one of the fastest-growing economies in the world, India needs quality healthcare for all its citizens, and undoubtedly it has made remarkable progress on the healthcare front. Many diseases, including smallpox and polio, have been eradicated. The country has also emerged as a hub for the manufacturing of generic drugs and medical tourism. Moreover, the government has started many commendable initiatives like Ayushman Bharat Yojana.

But the other side of the coin is that despite this progress, healthcare is underserved and under-consumed in India. Government hospitals are overcrowded and understaffed, whereas private hospitals are unaffordable for many needy people. Sadly, chronic diseases such as cardiovascular diseases, diabetes and cancer are the cause of about 50 per cent of all deaths in India. Furthermore, India has the second-largest geriatric population in the world. Imagine how difficult it would be for older people to visit hospitals or several doctors, quite possibly in different locations, to address their regular healthcare needs.

According to a Knowlede@Wharton article, for an average individual, 70 per cent of their healthcare needs can be met in the home environment. This can result in better health outcomes and lower medical costs for the patients. Over the last few years, India has witnessed the rapid rise of the home-based healthcare industry, and many organised, technology-led branded players are entering this industry. This is the story of one such player Portea.

Founded in 2013, Portea is India's largest and fastest-growing home healthcare company. By 2019, Portea had served more than 2.5 million customers and expanded its presence to 16 cities. During its brief journey, Portea has won various recognitions such as Health-tech Startup of the Year at the NDTV Unicorn Awards and Emerging Health Brand of the Year at the India Health Summit & Awards. Moreover, *Fortune India* has recognised Portea's co-founder and CEO, Meena Ganesh, as one of the 50 Most Powerful Women in Business, and *Forbes India* has called her W-Power Trailblazer.

According to media reports, Portea has received significant rounds of funding from many marquee investors, including Accel Partners, the World Bank's private lending arm IFC, Qualcomm Ventures, Alteria Capital, Ventureast, MEMG CDC Ventures, Sabre Partners and GrowthStory.

THE BEGINNING

Meena was born into a middle-class family. Owing to her father's job in the Indian Railways, she grew up across the country. After completing her schooling from a Kendriya Vidyalaya, she pursued her undergraduate degree in physics to become a nuclear physicist. But during her graduation, she realised that she didn't have the mentality to become a researcher, so she decided to pursue MBA.

After completing her MBA from IIM Calcutta, she worked with organisations like NIIT, PricewaterhouseCoopers and Microsoft. She also co-founded one of India's pioneering BPO companies, Customer Asset, which was acquired by ICICI. Then, she went on to become the CEO of Tesco's India centre. In 2008, along with her husband Krishnan Ganesh, she co-founded TutorVista, a leader in online education that eventually got acquired by the world's largest education company, Pearson.

While Meena was running TutorVista, her father was diagnosed with cancer. He was treated at the Manipal Hospital, one of the top hospitals in India, and was attended by the best doctors. But once he was discharged from the hospital, both Meena and her husband Krishnan had to run from pillar to post to get quality medical care for him. Unfortunately, in 2010, Meena lost her father to cancer. While taking care of him, she saw him struggle with multiple hospital visits that would take over two or three hours due to travel, traffic and hospital waiting times. During this tough period, she realised that the lack of affordable and quality home healthcare in India was a big problem that needed to be addressed.

By 2013, the acquisition of TutorVista was completed. While thinking about her next move, Meena recalled the challenges her father faced outside the hospital. She felt, by filling the void of the home healthcare system in India, she would be able to make a significant social impact. Hence, the journey of Portea began in June 2013 from a small office in Bengaluru.

THE BRAND NAME: PORTEA

For any consumer business, creating a strong brand identity is an integral aspect, and a large part of a brand's identity lies in the brand name.

Meena's vision has been to position her business as a trusted port of call for every healthcare need that an individual and their family members may have outside of hospital care. Also, when she started, she was clear about taking the business global. So, she wanted a brand name that sounded positive, tied up with her vision and had a broader meaning and international appeal.

Interestingly, there is a rare Brazilian flower called Portea. The name Portea sounds like the phrase 'port of call' and reflects positivity. So, Meena chose it as the brand name.

BUSINESS LESSONS

Many valuable lessons can be learnt from Portea's evolution as a brand. A few of them follow.

Have the humility for lifelong learning

One of the greatest thinkers and religious teachers, Jiddu Krishnamurti once said, 'There is no end to education. It is not that you read a book, pass an examination, and finish with education. The whole of life, from the moment you are born to the moment you die, is a process of learning.' Before starting Portea, Meena had worked at top positions at many renowned organisations. Furthermore, she had founded and sold two successful businesses. But instead of getting comfortable because of her past successes, she became curious to understand the field of healthcare, about which she didn't have much prior knowledge.

Six months before starting Portea, Meena began her learning process. She met a lot of people, including doctors, patients and leaders from the pharmaceutical and insurance sectors and medical equipment companies. This exercise helped her look at the problem in different forms and shapes.

India is one of the most populous countries in the world, so imagine the number of patients who would be deprived of medical care with the country's limited resources as a developing nation. For hospitals, the singular metric of profitability is the average revenue per operating bed, which depends on the average length of stay of a patient. Typically, hospitals make the maximum amount of money per patient in the first 48–72 hours of admission. So, both from the demand and profitability perspectives, it is essential for hospitals to enable a quick turnout of patients. But even after treatment at the hospital, many patients need care at home. Though big hospitals have extensively skilled human resources to work in the hospital environment, they don't have a trained workforce to serve patients at their homes. Meena realised that the home healthcare system has the potential to support the hospital system by becoming their extended arm.

India also has the second-largest geriatric population in the world. Nowadays, many children are moving to different cities and countries for jobs. By interacting with people who stay away from their parents, Meena found that they are always concerned about their family members' doctor visits, which are often missed or delayed. In fact, the people living in the same cities are constrained by time due to their office and travel schedules and find it challenging to manage multiple doctor visits for their family members. Looking at this problem, Meena felt that she could fill a significant void by providing home-based healthcare for older people. To cast its net wider, Portea introduced an NRI package. Under this, NRIs can sign up for customised in-home healthcare services for their relatives in India and get regular updates from the company.

India is seeing a rapid rise in chronic diseases. Chronic conditions are complicated and require a great deal of treatment, follow-ups and medication. So, people who suffer from one or more chronic conditions require ongoing medical attention. Managing a chronic disease along with a doctor's appointment and travel can overwhelm, exhaust and discourage a patient. Looking at this problem, Meena felt that the home healthcare system could be instrumental in helping these patients by providing primary care physicians and trained nurses at home.

In India, every city is different. To understand the challenges of people in different cities, Meena even travelled to multiple cities and worked with hospitals and doctors in various specialty areas to know more. This initial learning phase helped Meena in laying the foundation of Portea. But as every field is continuously evolving, Meena continues to learn from those around her. She has read all the books authored by Atul Gawande, an American surgeon and professor at Harvard Medical School. She has also read books from many other medical and healthcare practitioners, including those by Dr Eric Topol, an American cardiologist, geneticist and digital medicine researcher. Additionally, she has been an active member of various medical and healthcare associations and attends conferences to connect with and learn from multiple players in the ecosystem.

Portea's investors have also worked with many healthcare providers. So, Meena picks up opportunities to learn from the investors as well as their networks. As the concept of home healthcare is new in India, Meena has visited countries like the USA, the UK and Singapore to study models of home healthcare companies present there. By studying the home healthcare models of other countries, she found that while the home healthcare businesses receive ample private insurance support in developed countries like the USA, the same had not yet happened in India. Over time, Portea partnered with many insurance companies and is working on ways to support home healthcare service costs.

Meena says, 'As an entrepreneur, you face situations you have not encountered before. Have the willingness to learn from anybody and everybody.' The healthcare ecosystem from hospitals to doctors to patients to insurance and medical equipment companies is continuously evolving. To consistently match the wavelength of these evolving stakeholders, Meena keeps updating her knowledge. Her curiosity to learn and a powerful sense of determination have played an instrumental role in the growth of Portea.

Play to your strengths

Simon Sinek said, 'Spending too much time focused on others' strengths leaves us feeling weak. Focusing on our strengths is what makes us strong.' When Meena started Portea, though she didn't have a background in the medical field, she had experience in other areas like scaling up businesses, building large organisations, creating scalable technology infrastructure and forging partnerships. Meena's strengths in multiple business areas have helped her in establishing this new category in the country.

Unlike the high-margin business models of hospitals, home healthcare is a low-margin business model. So, it is a volume game. Looking at the various needs within the market and catering to a large number of patients with multiple small needs, the company has defined different revenue models, such as pay per visit and an annual package with facilities including regular health check-ups, doctor visits, regular nursing and other facilities. For special needs, the company has a few premium packages.

Unlike a hospital system where the patient visits a doctor, the home healthcare system requires the ability to handle last-mile logistics. One clinician has to visit multiple patients in a day. Now, to meet patients at different locations, clinicians have to travel optimally such that lesser time goes into travel and traffic and more time goes into seeing patients. Portea's app allows patients to book a service anytime, anywhere, and its technology platform assigns a qualified medical professional to a patient optimised based on geo-location, type of service requested and preferred time slot. Aggregate demand in their close vicinity helps medical professionals avoid long-distance travel and meet a greater number of patients in a shorter timespan.

In hospitals, people come to an office (the hospital) and work in a controlled environment. In the case of the home healthcare business, medical professionals go directly from their homes to the homes of patients. Portea uses technology to manage its remote workforce and standardise processes. All clinicians and field staff are monitored through an Android app on smartphones that the clinicians have to carry. While visiting existing patients, using the app, clinicians can access the patient's medical history, and check specific instructions from the consulting specialists. Clinicians use diagnostic tools to capture patient data and upload it through their smartphones onto an online medical record platform. Furthermore, Portea's patient care is divided into three levels. The work of a clinicians is overseen by subject matter experts who, in turn are supervised by Portea's Medical Director.

To become profitable, a business has to scale-up, and while scaling up, many companies compromise on quality standards. To overcome this, Portea has made various technology-based innovations. For instance, to enable patients to access their medical records anytime and from anywhere in the world, Portea's online patient portal provides electronic medical documentation. Another example is Portea's use of point-of-care devices and remote monitoring equipment at patients' homes to capture vitals such as blood pressure, temperature and blood glucose levels. Portea's platform then uses predictive analytics to analyse health trends. If the trend indicates that the patient's health is deteriorating, the platform alerts a doctor to monitor the patient. Also, back-end algorithms check for adverse drug reactions and provide an alert in case a patient's vitals cross internally set thresholds.

The medical ecosystem has multiple players such as hospitals, pathology labs, insurance companies, pharmaceutical companies and so on. Every player brings something different to the table and by combining offerings of all the players, unique offerings can be created for customers. Under the guidance of Meena, Portea has forged a wide range of partnerships within the ecosystem. These partnerships have allowed Portea to consolidate quality healthcare services under one roof. By October 2019, Portea was working with more than 75 leading hospital partners, 15 pharma majors and leading insurance companies in India. From the B2B customers' perspective, Portea has tied up with many corporates to take care of their employee's primary medical care. Based on synergies, Portea has also been partnering with many other industry players.

By delivering quality treatment at home with greater convenience and at a more effective cost, Portea has created a win-win situation for both hospitals and patients. Now, hospitals can serve more critical cases, and patients can fulfil many of their needs at home.

It takes a lot of time and effort to build trust in your brand

Jillian Michaels said, 'It's not about perfect. It's about effort. And when you bring that effort every single day, that's where transformation happens. That's how change occurs.' From a brand-building context, if you look closely, you would find that no trustworthy brand was perfect on day one. A lot of consistent effort by people behind the scenes is what makes a brand reliable.

Building a consumer brand is tough. Furthermore, creating a consumer healthcare brand is tougher than building an FMCG product brand. Healthcare is a very personal and emotive issue, and people take extra care in choosing a healthcare brand as compared to an FMCG brand of toothpaste or soap. The Indian home healthcare market is dominated by the unorganised sector, which provides sub-quality care and untrained professionals. So, one of the initial challenges for Portea was gaining the trust of the ecosystem. To build credibility, Meena first reached out to a few reputed hospitals for partnerships.

From a hospital's perspective, a patient needs time to recover well after the treatment. In many cases, especially those involving surgery, recovery happens over months, and as patients are at their homes, hospitals have no control over the recovery process. So, alignment with a branded partner like Portea that can provide quality service during the post-hospitalisation recovery process is an excellent value addition for hospitals. When Meena started this business, many hospitals were looking for a partner that could provide home-based healthcare as per their defined protocols. But, as Portea was an unknown brand then, hospitals were concerned about Portea's capabilities and wary of an alliance that could dilute the brand of the hospital if something went wrong. Hospitals were also concerned that Portea might transfer their patients to other hospitals.

To clear the doubts that the hospitals were having, rather than starting multiple offerings at one time, Portea started with only one offering—physiotherapy. It also showed its systems to hospital management to show them that patients were not being transferred to any other hospitals. The initial hospitals went through a lot of due diligence before trusting Portea. Eventually, a couple of them agreed to do a six-month pilot and referred Portea to a few of their patients. Meena made sure that the quality of the service would be such that people would vouch for the brand. The feedback of customers (patients) was positive, and reputed hospitals, such as Manipal Hospital and Columbia Asia, both in Bengaluru, became Portea's first two partners. Because of these reputed partnerships and the positive word-of-mouth publicity from patients, the process for gaining more such partnerships became a bit easier. Soon, more hospitals started gaining the confidence to partner with Portea.

Simultaneously, Portea started performance-based marketing through online channels such as Google and Facebook. As people were already looking for services like physiotherapy at home, the company began getting customers directly. Soon, Portea began two other offerings—doctors on call and nursing care at home. From the third year of its operations, Portea started contacting specialist doctors for partnerships and over time, it launched many new offerings, such as providing medical equipment, diagnostic services, critical care and chronic disease management. Meanwhile, the company also began expanding its operations to other cities.

In 2016, Portea rolled out its first TV campaign. One of India's first commercials on home healthcare was aired on 32 channels across the country. This commercial showcased that while medical treatment can be obtained in a hospital, it is widely acknowledged that a patient heals best at home under the care of a home healthcare professional and around the people that the patients are most comfortable with. As Portea was building a new category, this commercial created a lot of awareness and transformed the way people saw home healthcare and Portea. Interestingly, many ecosystem players, prospective partners and customers started looking at Portea as a credible player. Soon, Portea started getting customers through word of mouth and referrals by hospitals, doctors and other ecosystem players. Besides, the team used traditional means of marketing like print, radio and outdoor campaigns to create awareness.

As more and more people started becoming aware of the brand and its offerings, Portea started many business development initiatives with its partners that included several NGOs. It organised health camps at apartment complexes and corporate offices. As part of these camps, doctors provide advice and necessary medicines. The company also holds blood tests and consultations based on test reports. Moreover, it distributes free medical kits to NGOs and organises health talks and camps for senior citizens.

In any field, especially in healthcare, providing good quality at affordable prices and doing all of this at scale is a considerable challenge. Though Portea has built a powerful brand and awareness around its offerings, it has been cautious about its expansion from both a quality and a unit economics perspective. In the near future, it would be interesting to see how the brand evolves to manage the rising demand for its offerings.

Find your product–market fit

Steve Blank said, 'Customer discovery is the process of translating a founder's vision for the company into hypotheses about each component of the business model and creating a set of experiments to test each hypothesis.' From day one, Portea was clear that it is not going to compete with hospitals. It doesn't provide specialists or emergency care, the core value proposition of hospitals. Instead, it complements hospitals by becoming their extended arm for offerings like better quality post-operative and primary care at homes.

From the market perspective, Portea focused on the middle-class segment in tier-1 and tier-2 cities, especially the ones with a population of more than a million people. The company also prioritised cities where premium and big hospitals were present, as the presence of these hospitals signified that people in the city spent money on healthcare. Due to various reasons ranging from the low level of income to lower profitability to people being sceptical about trying home medical care, the company has still not focused on tier-3 cities.

From an offerings perspective, Portea provides geriatric care, post-operative care, palliative care, primary care, physiotherapy, collection of lab samples, home delivery of medicines and medical equipment for hire. Within the same market, different customers value different things. Some people demand the lowest possible price, some want a dedicated service relationship, and some are looking for the best technology or brand. Uncovering the full truth about customers' preferences requires multiple experiments. To validate their hypotheses, Portea's team has done numerous experiments. Some experiments didn't meet customers' demands in terms of pricing and service relationship. But a few of them have evolved into successful programmes. Let's have a look at a few hypotheses and programmes created around them.

After intensive intervention, many hospitals keep patients in the ICU because they need extensive monitoring. However, there is no active intervention. A lot of hospitals now feel that this period is better served at home if patients get proper care.

To help serve this need, Portea started offering an ICU-at-home solution, which provides monitoring, nursing, ventilators and other equipment. Also, an emergency physician is made available to talk to the patient's caregivers.

The population of senior citizens in the country is increasing, and many of them have one or more chronic conditions. To manage the health of senior citizens at home, Portea has launched a membership programme called Portea Health Prime. Usually, the younger generation wants to pay for such a service so that their parents are well taken care of. The package includes an emergency alert device, a specific doctor who continuously monitors the health needs of elders, and a health manager who ensures that a customised healthcare plan is delivered and implemented.

Nowadays, children move away for their careers, and the extended family lives far away. Hence, along with health issues, senior citizens face the problem of loneliness. Also, the concept of old-age homes is still not widely accepted in India. So, Portea's membership programme includes additional benefits such as social gatherings, workshops, events and communities suitable for elders.

People suffering from chronic diseases like diabetes need critical care at home. For patients suffering from chronic diseases, Portea has started multiple specialised programmes. For instance, for diabetes patients, Portea has launched a one-of-its-kind programme—InControl—which puts in place a comprehensive diabetes care plan, provides the necessary equipment for monitoring and offers one-on-one health coaching. With an annual subscription, a patient gets a free glucometer, an unlimited supply of test strips, and the right health coaching through a certified counsellor for one year. This programme also brings together diabetologists and nutrition counsellors to a technology platform where they can remotely monitor patients' conditions and work with patients to bring forth positive health outcomes.

Another vital area that Portea has been able to cater to is home-based healthcare for the infant and adolescent age groups with more critical medical conditions such as palsy, delayed milestones and Down's Syndrome. Taking children with any of these ailments to the doctor time and again is challenging for parents, especially when one of the parents is travelling or in office and the other has to manage work, home and children all on their own. Thus, Portea provides services like long-term physiotherapy, attendants, nursing, vaccination, etc. at home.

Portea also offers a carefully designed Kanga and Roo programme. Under this, the company assigns a medically trained caregiver to help the mother with after-delivery care and newborn baby care. About 7 per cent of Portea's patients are below 14 years of age, and this segment is growing faster than the company's total patient base.

Similarly, by looking at the various customer segments and their specific needs, Portea has implemented many other programmes.

Match and create talent for your needs

One of the biggest problems in expanding home healthcare services in India is the lack of a skilled workforce. India has a decent supply of healthcare talent, but this talent is trained to work in controlled and organised environments like hospitals. Working in the home healthcare industry needs many skills that are different from the hospital system. Unfortunately, the Indian education system currently does not have a structured training programme for home healthcare.

In a home, the power equation is very different from the power equation in a hospital. In a hospital, a patient is surrounded by medical practitioners and takes their directions seriously, but in a home setup, a clinician is surrounded by many family members. The clinician at home not only has to build relationships with family members but also has to act with authority if the patient is not taking their instructions seriously.

In some cases, patients may have limited communication abilities, significant physical and mental ailments, and other challenging situations. Nurses at home have to work with these patients daily, often for hours. They need to empathise and interact with patients in a way that is both healthy and respectful. But the response from a patient can often be thankless and depressing. Even then, the nurses have to maintain their patience and positivity. Unlike in a hospital setting, nurses in home settings don't have a head nurse or a doctor directing their every move. They have to take requests and directions from the patients at times, but they also need the ability to make independent decisions, work efficiently, and act swiftly in emergencies. Similarly, medical practitioners have to face many other challenges in a home environment.

Meena noticed several gaps in skill set between the available talent and healthcare professionals who are the right fit for the home healthcare environment. To succeed in this journey, she needed to hire people whose skill sets could be matched with the needs, and simultaneously, she had to create new talent. Meena reached out to her network to find people who could help her in laying the foundation of talent and culture. One of the initial persons to join the team was Dr Udaya Maiya, whom Meena had known for over a decade. Dr Maiya is a very senior healthcare practitioner and has played an instrumental role in Portea, by supervising hiring, designing customised training programmes and building Portea's relationships with healthcare service providers. To get the first 200 people in the company, Meena personally interviewed thousands of candidates and selected the ones with a great learning attitude along with the required skills.

Over time, Portea has also forged partnerships with organisations like National Skill Development Corporation (NSDC) to source talent. NSDC selects the nursing attendants from rural and semi-urban areas and sends them to Portea. After a primary interview, the candidates are trained on etiquette, hygiene, behaviour and customer care. Furthermore, many MBBS doctors who used to work as supporters of specialised doctors in hospitals prefer to join home healthcare companies like Portea because of the independence and responsibility they get in this model.

Within a period of six years, Portea's team had grown to 4,000 team members consisting of doctors, nurses, physiotherapists, caregivers, administrators and engineers. A large number of employees, such as caregivers and medical practitioners, offer direct clinical services at home and are predominantly mobile. Many employees perform supervisory activities such as oversight and assessments, and this group is partially mobile, splitting time between the office and patients' homes. A small percentage of people contribute to administrative activities and work from the office. As people come from different backgrounds, the company runs an intensive induction programme and regular training programmes for participants with varying levels of knowledge and roles to play.

While India faces an unemployment crisis, ironically, the home healthcare industry is facing a shortage of skilled workers. Meena says, 'As a fast-growing company, Portea is always looking out for great talent, but to maintain the customer experience, it maintains rigorous hiring standards.' She further adds, 'There is a lot of scope for business growth, but the company has not been able to scale-up many offerings because of the shortage of talent that is needed to meet the demand at the required unit economics.'

India has an established ecosystem of family doctors and hospitals. These players have significant resources and industry experience, but they can't fulfil the need for home healthcare. Surprisingly, for ages, the market was filled with many unorganised players who were providing fragmented services to customers. But then suddenly, a new player—Portea—came and disrupted the industry. You might be wondering why new players with limited resources disrupt the industry while established players can't.

As Harvard professor Clayton Christensen said, 'The reason why it is so difficult for existing firms to capitalize on disruptive innovations is that their processes and their business model that make them good at the existing business actually make them bad at competing for the disruption.' Thus, Meena's journey of creating Portea gives hope that even without the relevant background, with determination and hard work, a new player can disrupt an industry and create a billion-dollar opportunity.

MEENA GANESH

Advice from Meena Ganesh

- Anybody looking for creating a startup should look for large unsolved problems and the massive impact that could be made through the solution.
- Keeping an eye on the competition is essential, but keeping an eye on your customers is necessary. How they are evolving, whether they are willing to pay for your offering, are you relevant to their lives as their needs are changing—these are a few essential questions that every entrepreneur should ask themself.
- Anybody who is entering the workplace and starting to build their career should look at the job description (JD) only as a direction. A JD should not be considered a limiting factor. Think about what more you can do to make a difference to the company. Think about how you can stand out of the crowd, not by speaking louder, but by doing something valuable.
- Change in technology and business models is very much accelerated now. So, if you have to remain relevant ten years from now, you have to keep reinventing yourself by learning new skills and doing things that are outside of your comfort zone.
- A relevant brand is the one that is missed by its consumers when it is not there. So, an entrepreneur should focus on building a brand that plays an essential role in people's lives.

Acknowledgments

This book would not have been possible without the advice, motivation and support of the incredible people who contributed immensely to my endeavour.

I would first and foremost like to thank my wife Pooja. When I started writing this book, our daughter Yashvi was six months old. Pooja singlehandedly took care of Yashvi, so that I could work on my writing. In whatever limited time she got, she motivated me to focus on this book. On weekends and holidays, as I utilised every minute of my time to complete this project, she sacrificed her plans and kept my morale high. She made me believe that I could do it. I am also thankful to Yashvi for becoming an important reason for me to write this book.

I will always be grateful to my friend Manish Pandey, who has always motivated me in my endeavours. Thank you, Manish, for your valuable support. I sincerely appreciate Rohit Chanana for being an extraordinary supporter of my entire journey.

A big thank you to Anand Lunia, Dr Anand Deshpande, Rajiv Prakash, Venky Iyer, Mangesh Khunte, Sasha Mirchandani, Sandeep Singhal, Ajay Hattangdi and Tajdar Khan for encouraging me to write my second book. I am genuinely grateful to Pramod Jejurikar, Abhijit Jejurikar, R. Sriram, Sameer Arora, Vineet Malhotra, Mahalakshmi Ajaykumar, Gaurav Mendiratta, Shabnam Khan and Taruna Upadhyaya for believing in me and pushing me to achieve my true potential. Also, many thanks to M.D. Agrawal. He has always encouraged me in my journey. I am deeply grateful to Arpit Jain, Manish Acharya, Achintya Goyal and Devendra Khatri for their invaluable assistance.

I am grateful to Nishant Sengupta, for his invaluable help in reviewing my write-ups. His feedback on the early drafts helped me a lot in improving the stories. One more person I would like to thank for his inputs and feedback is my friend Abhishek Boharpi. He read all the chapters enthusiastically and shared his thoughts.

Thanks to Rahul Tewari, Milap Shah, K. Ganesh, Shripad Nadkarni, Ajit Nagral, Vibhu Nagral, Vinay Joy and Swarup Nanda, for always supporting everything that I do. I am also thankful to my sister Honey and my friend Arvind Kishore for encouraging me to pursue such meaningful goals.

Thank you to the people I interviewed for sharing their stories. They gave me their valuable time and shared their inputs with a lot of passion and patience. At Epigamia, thanks to Rohan Mirchandani and Siddarth Menon; at BigBasket, thanks to Hari Menon; at Super 30 thanks to Anand Kumar; at PolicyBazaar, thanks to Yashish Dahiya, Aman Dhall and Akshay Kumar; at Zoomcar, thanks to Greg Moran, Varun Jha, Anish Behera and Chandan Mohapatra; at Hidesign thanks to Dilip Kapur and Dipen Desai; at Portea, thanks to Meena Ganesh; at Josh Talks, thanks to Supriya Paul, Deepak Nanda and Mitul Lall; at ShareChat, thanks to Ankush Sachdeva, Farid Ahsan and Preeti Nair; at OYO, thanks to Ritesh Agarwal, Malavikka Sharma, and Karen Annunciation; at Quikr, thanks to Pranay Chulet, Sonali Madbhavi and Harinee Sivaprakasam.

I am thankful to Prashant Sinha and his team for creating beautiful caricatures of all the founders covered in the book. I express my utmost gratitude to the entire team at TV18 Broadcast

Limited (CNBC TV18) for publishing the first edition of this book. I am also grateful to Westland Books for recognising the potential of my work and agreeing to publish this edition. A special thanks to Karthika V.K. for her invaluable guidance and unwavering support. I deeply appreciate the tremendous support of Sonia Madan in this project. Thank you, Sonia, for making this book so much better with your thoughtful edits. I also want to thank Avdyushka Gupta for her round of edits and proofreading.

Finally, I would like to thank many others who have helped me in shaping my journey. I am thankful to Manak Singh and Zankhana Kaur for giving me an opportunity to work at TiE. I am also grateful to Vispy Doctor, Hareesh Tibrewala, Sanjay Mehta, Anuj Jain and Mohit Dubey, for inspiring me to build a career in marketing. Thanks to Pravin Gandhi, Dr Annurag Batra, Sourav Majumdar, Hariharan M. and Prakash Iyer, for inspiring me to become an author. Thanks to Raj Nair, Arun Diaz, Pramod Gothi, Sumir Verma, Manu Parpia, Mahesh Krishnamurti, Lakshmi Pratury, Utkarsh Amitabh, Gautam Sharma, Supam Maheshwari, Kunwer Sachdev, Nitin Seth, Rahul Gupta, Ajay Aggarwal, Vivek Singh, Aashika Jain, Prakash Hemdev, Vijay Francis, Ramesh Ramakrishnan and Nachiket Deshpande for encouraging me to pursue meaningful goals.